# Dual Mission

*A True Crime Memoir*

*A Secret Service Agent's Battle with the New York Mafia!*

*...And Other International Crime Intrigue*

Nino Perrotta

BEST SELLER
PUBLICATIONS LLC

Maryland, USA

Best Seller Publications, LLC

BestSellerPublications.com

BestSellerPublications@gmail.com


Library of Congress Cataloging-in-Publication Data

Names: Pasquale Nino Perrotta, 1967-Present.
Title: Dual Mission
Description: Trade paperback edition. | Maryland : Best Seller Publications, LLC, 2024.
Identifiers:
          ISBN: 978-0-9642997-2-6 (softcover)
          Library of Congress Control Number: 2023923929

Subjects: Career highlights of a US Secret Service Agent who investigated the Gambino crime family, international fugitives, and other criminal rings. | BISAC: TRU003000

Printed in the United States of America

## Acknowledgements

I very much appreciate the support I've received in making *Dual Mission* a well-crafted read. Many thanks to the publisher, Best Seller Publications, LLC, for providing editorial support and the many beta readers, including Hillary Blackton, Connie Cosler, and Ray Villemez, who offered their insightful suggestions. I also want to acknowledge the loyalty and, at times, life-saving support of my many law enforcement partners and colleagues who helped me become the best Special Agent I could be.

*Dedication*

I dedicate this book to the men and women of the United States Secret Service who successfully manage the daily challenges the job brings to each of you and your loved ones. I also share this dedication with my son, Antonio, and daughter, Valentina. I hope that you both learn a few "interesting" things about your dad while reading this book and the challenges life can present when you push yourself and others toward a higher cause.

Quotation

*"The only way to fight the Mafia is with the law in one hand and the truth in the other."*

— Magistrate Giovanni Falcone

# Table of Contents

# 1  Foreword

The U.S. Secret Service is a dual mission agency, charged with safeguarding our nation's financial infrastructure and protecting high-profile political figures, such as the U.S. president and visiting heads of state/government.

The following chapters are delivered in the author's voice and cover his many career highlights, including successful investigations of check fraud, bank robberies, and a Mafia-operated "calling card scheme" that scammed large telecommunications corporations and the public out of $94 million.

Special Agent Perrotta's tenacious investigations led to the arrest of the 1990s Mafia crime boss John Gotti Junior and roughly 40 mob associates for racketeering. Special Agent Perrotta's investigations also ensnared the Cy Young Award winning and former Major League Baseball pitcher Denny McLain, who was involved in such organized crime.

In addition, this memoir follows Special Agent Perrotta's missions in Romania, Bulgaria, and Italy, including his relentless pursuit of an international fugitive.

*Dual Mission* would not be complete without introducing the foundation of Nino Perrotta: his familial background, his upbringing, and his rise in the ranks, culminating to U.S. Secret Service Senior Special Agent.

One quality Nino possesses is that he has been, and remains, loyal to country, the mission, and friends. Nino always conducted professional investigations, found the criminal, and made consequential arrests.

A consistent theme throughout his 25-year career in this profession is the extreme dedication and patriotism of those with whom he served. Nino has worked alongside the very best people in law enforcement, bar none.

## 2   The Fugitive and Me

At the age of 7, I always played the cowboy—the "good guy." Little did I know, as an adult I would be a Special Agent in the United States Secret Service investigating and capturing international fugitives and Mafia kingpins.

I grew up in New York City, where I learned the survival instincts that prepared me to work in one of the most inhospitable and dangerous places for an agent: Bulgaria. After a 2-year assignment in Rome, Italy, I was relocated in 2002 to Sophia, Bulgaria, where contract killings were common and the price tag on life was cheap.

A suspicious nature served one well in this country. Akin to riding the subways of New York as a young teenager in the 1980s, I learned to maintain a situational awareness as if my head were on a swivel. In New York I was never caught off guard, lest I be a victim of a mugging or random act of street violence. Bulgaria was similar, except complacency could result in a shortened life.

My mission in Bulgaria was to locate and apprehend a fugitive known as Petar "Peter" Simenov. He was at the time a top priority of the United States Secret

Service, which wanted his safe return to the U.S. to face charges related to the distribution of counterfeit U.S. currency in the New York region. He had been successfully investigated, charged, and arrested by Secret Service agents. However once released on bail, he absconded to his native country of Bulgaria.

I was the first agent to establish a permanent investigative unit and remain in Bulgaria for an extended period. At the time, I was a single man with few material possessions and no binding relationships or commitments. The U.S. State Department assisted me with housing and required paperwork to serve as an attaché to the American Embassy. Once in the country, I needed to be extremely careful since my target was well connected to Bulgarian and Russian organized crime syndicates.

If I were going to be successful in my pursuit of Peter Simenov, I needed to determine whom I could trust and what networks I needed to penetrate to reach the only acceptable outcome: sending this international fugitive back to New York City to answer for his crimes before a U.S. magistrate judge.

The station chief, Ralph, taught me who's who in the Bulgarian political, social, and criminal arenas. The Bulgarian police were, in many cases, an extension of the organized crime syndicates that co-governed the country. Ralph led me toward those in government who were willing to support the interests of the United States. The ability to hit the ground running and know who to work with was crucial to my mission. The Bulgarian police and government could not be trusted. Trust had to be parceled out cautiously and vetted continuously.

I was charged with gaining the professional trust of a select few in government. To vet Bulgarian police and government officials, I coordinated meetings at various cafés and restaurants throughout the city. I also cultivated confidential informants who came from the private and public sectors, as well as society's underbelly—the criminal element.

I took every advantage to ensure my "friends" served as a set of eyes and ears on the ground for my protection. Through my contacts, I had my finger on the pulse of the city and exploited my status as an American diplomat in case I needed to vacate in a hurry.

Like everything I did, there was both a reason for and a method to it. Going out for the night was no different. I prepared for the nightlife by carefully selecting my clothing. My attire consisted of dark pants, and shirt underneath some sort of black leather jacket, which served to insulate and conceal my weapon.

My Sig Sauer 230, a .380-caliber handgun, was absolutely beautiful and quite compact. It was flawless. Once dressed and ready to go out, I was always confident. Why not? I was young, in shape, and dressed like a million bucks. However, there was one hurdle between the business of cultivating a network of informants and entering the forum in which I operated: the nightclub bouncers.

All the nightclubs in Sophia were staffed with menacing bouncers. These hulking men had a combination of wrestling and martial arts experience in addition to their bulky physique. They were intimidating and effective at their jobs, or so I thought. The bouncers physically checked patrons for weapons prior to entering the clubs and no one ever dared challenge them.

During the 1990s, a great deal of violence arose in Bulgaria. Turf wars in the streets of Sophia were commonplace. In an effort to prevent violence inside and outside the club, bouncers physically searched each patron. At first, whenever I planned on going to the clubs, I avoided the consequences of these pat downs by making a pit stop and leaving my weapon at my apartment, fearing it would be discovered and taken from me. I then devised a way to conceal my weapon based on a discernable pattern of their searches. The bouncers were either poorly trained or their failure to be thorough was deliberate. In previous experiences being patted down, I noticed that the bouncers did not perform a hands-on inspection of the groin. They intentionally avoided hand to groin contact, either because of bravado or homophobia. I knew then how to exploit their inhibitions. I took advantage that they would never dare touch or feel another man's most sacred place. So, I placed my Sig Sauer 230 in my waistband, positioning the weapon dead center over my crotch. It was a risky move at worst, an uncomfortable one at best.

I tested them by walking to the head of the line with a confidence bordering on arrogance. My demeanor, combined with their inhibitions to search all of me led the bouncer into believing I had nothing to hide. If the gun moved even a bit, it would undoubtedly slip and fall through my pants leg onto the floor and potentially at the feet of the gorilla in front of me.

My actions were successful. Each and every time thereafter, my Sig resided next to my privates when entering a Bulgarian club. The weapon gave me a little protection, but my Sig was nothing more than a slingshot to what those folks had for fire power. This was a country where most of the Mafia bodyguards carried automatic weapons and used snipers to execute contract killings. The going rate to pay a sniper during the 1990s was between 5,000 and 50,000 euros. The amount of payment was dependent on how highly the target was rated. It was a risk-based approach to murder and quite common.

Bulgarian criminal organizations used a deliberate, albeit callous, decision-making process to carry out contract killings. They weighed the cost of killing an individual versus the level of scrutiny, loss of business, or public attention it would garner. At the time, I do not believe I represented a serious enough threat, or was even annoying enough to anyone, to be targeted for assassination. I did, however, gain some notoriety with the criminal element given my identity as a Secret Service agent with the sole purpose of locating the counterfeiting fugitive, Peter Simenov.

My routine visits to nightclubs were in full stride. I was armed and ready to move on a suspect. I noticed a young man, tall and blond. He was standing at a crowded bar waiting to be served. He fit the physical description of my fugitive.

I approached the bar while he conversed in Bulgarian with a beautiful woman. After a few minutes of scanning the crowd, while keeping him under close watch, I motioned for the bartender. I asked for a whiskey, a Jack Daniels straight up. It caught the man's attention.

He turned toward me, and I saw that he gave me a glance over, but did not say a word. I did not hesitate. I said in a commanding yet subdued voice, "How are you, Peter? My name is Nino, and I work for an organization you are very familiar with…the United States Secret Service."

I felt a tremendous sense of satisfaction. My mission and sole objective for being in Bulgaria had just hit a home run. I was moving forward. I went to bed that night with my Sig Sauer 380 tucked safely under my pillow and fell asleep knowing Peter Simenov had been found and would serve justice.

## 3  Growing Up Italian Near the Mob

To gain a better understanding of who Nino Perrotta is, it is important to know my Italian roots and how I grew from a kid into a young man.

We begin with the background of my parents in "the old country"—Italy, the birthplace of my mother, Luigina (Gina) Falco, and my father, Antonio (Tony) Perrotta. They married and lived in a small town of 1,900 residents about 35 km northeast of Naples.

After my parents' wedding, they cared for my grandmother Luisa Gallo Falco. Grandmother Luisa raised my mother as a single parent and widower. Her husband, my grandfather, died by suicide when Luisa was pregnant. Allegedly, he was falsely accused of theft at a market. By the time the real thief was apprehended, my grandfather—while in prison—slit his throat.

Grandmother Luisa did everything for her daughter, Gina, including sending her to Naples to get an education and learn the skills of a seamstress. This commitment to family and the drive to succeed against the odds has descended through the Perrotta family tree to this day.

My father and mother came to New York with virtually nothing. They had no money, no job, and very few prospects. What they did have in abundance was intense hope and an unyielding dream. This inspiration had been passed along by our aunts and uncles who had arrived on American soil years prior.

I was born in 1967, a year after my parents entered the United States as newlyweds. We lived in the Bronx with my grandmother's sister in a small apartment on the top floor over a bar called Scotty's. The 1960s were challenging times for my parents. My mother, Gina, worked as a seamstress in a sweatshop making wedding gowns. My father, Tony, was a day laborer.

I was the first of three children: my younger brother, Antonio "Tony," and my younger sister, Rosina, followed. In the early years, my grandmother and great-aunt took turns caring for me while my parents worked tirelessly to gain a footing in America. I spent my days in the apartment as my grandmother worked the midnight shift in a factory.

I was a difficult kid, always getting into trouble at home and in school. In retrospect, I was functioning with undiagnosed and unmedicated attention-deficit/hyperactivity disorder (ADHD). To this day, I have an abundance of energy. To others, I may appear as if I'm bouncing off the walls. I noticed anything and everything around me. It was a gift that served me well as an agent needing to be on guard with complete situational awareness at all times. But before I learned how to manage and exploit my awareness on any one thing, as a kid my ADHD resulted in my getting hit by cars; thankfully, slow-moving ones. In two incidents, I was a pedestrian and not paying attention to the thing that mattered—two-ton cars. Fortunately, I came away from both instances unscathed.

I was also a tough kid. When not getting screamed at by my parents, I was in the middle of some street ruckus or fistfight. Often the cause was my trying to stop some punk from bullying someone less capable. I have many scars and broken bones that serve as a road map to my youthful vigor and over-the-top idealism.

My childhood fantasies typically were acted out by pretending to be a cowboy who saved the day, or a policeman fighting the bad guys. As I grew older, my interest in helping those in need only grew stronger.

I have fond memories of our family parties where everyone—my aunts, uncles, and cousins—would get together for birthdays, First Communions, confirmations, any reason to gather in the kitchen to prepare old-style recipes and eat course after course. I took in every aspect of a room full of Italian immigrants: the talks about the old country, American politics, sports, and the hardships of running an Italian deli, which became the family business.

These family gatherings were wonderful—delicious food, laughter, and the games my cousins and I played, always involving toy guns and fireworks. One morning before a family party while my parents were still asleep, I wanted to see the effects a firecracker had on a plywood playhouse that I had built in our basement. The experiment was a success! Of sorts anyway. The fuse worked; there was an explosion; and the playhouse was obliterated. The downside of this victory was that the deafening blast echoed throughout our home. The firecracker went off with a resounding boom, followed by a cloud of smoke. I was so happy, but my joy was short-lived. Behind the cloud of smoke appeared my father, who, having jumped out of his bed from a deep slumber, ran downstairs to the basement in his Fruit-of-the-Looms with belt in hand. I got the beating of my life. Trust me, I learned two lessons that morning: first, a single firecracker did pack the necessary punch, but more importantly, witnessing an explosion is better suited outdoors.

Being raised in a predominantly Italian neighborhood, with family members all speaking Italian, I spoke Italian fluently and would get embarrassed whenever challenged to speak English. My behavioral issues worsened as the neighborhood changed over time to mostly English-speaking residents.

The language barrier became evident when I started school. I had a poor command of English. As a result, I was held back in the first grade, and academics did not come easily for me throughout my forthcoming school years.

Coming from a large, immigrant family, I was on the receiving end of hand-me-downs. I hated wearing my cousins' clothes, but I had no say. My older cousins, Pete and Pat, wore clothing that was in style in the 1960s. By the time they were recycled to me, they were extremely outdated and often did not fit well. At school, I was embarrassed and teased in the early 1980s for wearing bell-bottoms and other bygone styles.

I often fought back verbally and physically. The taunting and ridicule only led me into more trouble and a front-row seat in the principal's office. My parents had no idea how to manage me, so they removed me from public school and placed me in a private Catholic school.

In contrast, my parents provided me a lifetime of education one can never get in the finest schools. I learned the value of honest hard work by watching them work themselves to near exhaustion, day in and day out, as they doggedly worked while raising three children. I learned the meaning of integrity by watching my father always doing the right thing for his wife, children, and others.

Above all, I learned the true meaning of loyalty by my reflection upon their marriage. They were, and remain, extremely loyal to each other. My parents laid the groundwork for who I am today by their daily actions and, in particular, a decision they made in 1976. I was 9-years-old and remember an excitement in the air at home. My mother and father put up their entire life's savings and purchased a local delicatessen in Mount Vernon, New York.

The deli, called Mercurio Delicatessen, proved to be a great investment, and my experience with it instilled life lessons that would prove essential as a future Secret Service agent. After a few prosperous years, my folks relocated the deli down the block by purchasing a three-story building that my uncle, Mario, refurbished for them. My parents would never again pay rent. It was the American dream. And they proudly renamed the new deli Perrotta's Salumeria, the Italian word equivalent to Perrotta's Delicatessen. My folks wanted patrons to feel as if they entered an authentic Italian deli, similar to ones in the old country.

My assignment for the summer was to remove jars off 80 feet of shelving, 8 feet high, clean the shelves, then restock the items. It took me the entire summer, while my work underwent inspections from my father, who was simply "a hard ass on steroids." To him nothing was ever good enough. We battled throughout my entire childhood and young adulthood on everything from cleanliness of shelves to politics, friends, and work at the deli. In retrospect, the fact we lived and worked in close proximity all the time allowed us this tough but very unique experience. He was a true workhorse. My father enjoyed nothing more than a 14 to 16-hour workday, 7 days a week.

Everyone in the family worked in the deli. My mother was a tremendous salesperson, even though she never studied sales nor read a business book. She was a natural. It was something to watch her methodically lure the customer into a conversation about a particular cheese or cut of meat. She sprinkled this dialogue with stories of her childhood back in Italy. Once customers were hooked, she would subtly turn toward me and wink.

From behind the counter in my parents' deli, I learned many of the skills a good investigator needs: observation, interaction with the public, negotiation, anticipating people's needs, and identifying their weak spots and motivations.

Whenever the Mount Vernon police came in for a sandwich, I stared at their uniforms, badges, and guns. I engaged them by sharing my experiences tangling with neighborhood delinquents.

As my siblings and I grew and were more able to help, our responsibilities increased. We received recognition and were rewarded based on how hard we worked. Since I was the oldest child, I was expected to work the hardest. I had many responsibilities. One such job was to watch patrons and deter those few who attempted to steal food and merchandise. In later years, I occasionally redirected drunks and disruptive mentally ill persons out of the store.

Another significant threat to our livelihood was the proximity of two strip clubs, both located just a stone's throw away from our family business.

The owner of one of the clubs, Tony, was a short, stocky man in his early 40s. To a kid, he seemed old. He exhibited a large chest and biceps like a weightlifter, and wore an unnatural-looking dark hairpiece. Tony was street savvy, a quality one can only get by living in certain inner-city environments. In keeping with stereotypes, Tony was indeed connected with certain elements of the criminal underworld. He also spent a lot of time and money in our deli.

I found Tony intriguing. He always wore black pants, black shirts, and lots of gold chains and a pinky ring. In the summer, he wore silk t-shirts; in the winter, he wore thin, custom-fit black leather jackets. When he paid for his purchases, he pulled out a wad of crisp 100-dollar bills from his front pocket. My father loved Tony's business. The club owner purchased large chunks of Parmigiano-Reggiano cheese, dry sausage, and provolone cheese on a weekly basis.

One day, Tony came in with his Filipino girlfriend, an ex-stripper, and asked my father to cut him a piece of provolone cheese. Of course, this request made my father very happy. Dad walked to the rear of the deli, pulled out a 4-foot-long wedge of well-aged "Auricchio" provolone, and started by placing his large knife on the wedge ready to cut a 1-inch-thick piece.

Tony stopped him with a mere facial expression, so my dad moved the knife for a wider wedge. Tony continued to signal with just his demeanor and a slight squint to expand the desired chunk. My father became visibly happier. The chunk of cheese that was eventually cut was very impressive and quite expensive.

Tony was connected with organized crime, and word on the street was, he had local politicians in his pocket. If you needed a loan or wanted to place a bet on your favorite team, Tony and his associates were the ones you needed to see. In the summer, he and other similar-looking men stood outside the strip club and leaned against new Cadillacs discussing business.

I earned an invaluable education working in the deli that no textbook or academy can impart. I had a front-row seat to real-life wise guys. They came in and out of the deli with such regularity that the colorful language they used and the animated way they carried themselves became commonplace for me. I saw and listened to their interactions and witnessed them during unguarded moments as they waited for my dad to slice the mortadella. This was my introduction to the Mafia and it shaped my approach to dealing with the underworld. My observations eventually helped me become a "mob buster."

## 4  Becoming an Investigator: Rising in the Ranks

My break into law enforcement finally came in the early 1990s in New York. I was the first in my family to earn a college degree in the United States. I graduated from Fordham University with a bachelor's degree in political science and a minor in philosophy. I was newly married to a woman I met at Fordham, and I had completed a 6-month U.S. Army Military Intelligence Officer's Basic Course at Fort Huachuca, Arizona. Any one of these milestones, let alone the combination of them, was reason enough to celebrate. Most satisfying, however, was the day I received a letter advising me to report to the Rockland County Police and Public Safety Academy. I had secured a probationary position as an investigator with the Bronx District Attorney, Detective Investigator (DI) Squad.

For the next 6 months, I reported daily to the police academy in Pomona, New York, where I further developed the investigative skill sets necessary to take on the New York Mafia. My life experiences growing up around "wise guys" complemented the technical training received in the army and at the police academy.

Soon after receiving my commission as a second lieutenant in the United States Army Reserves, I completed my first phase of training in Fort

Huachuca, Arizona. During this period, I moved from one training academy to the next. It was here, while dealing with the crushing amounts of information and a rigid classroom structure, that I was presented with a horrendous moral situation, a leadership challenge that was obviously not part of the formal training.

A female classmate who was a West Point graduate became a close friend. She was married to a United States Army Special Ops lieutenant who was in the Middle East at the time. One evening while returning to her apartment, she was raped by the class coordinator, a first lieutenant who was part of the training staff. Despite having been expelled from West Point previously for allegedly doing the same horrific act of violence, he still managed to get an Officer Candidate School (OCS) commission. My lady friend and I were in the unfortunate class to have him as an instructor.

After this violent incident occurred, my friend called me in distress. All I heard was her crying and muttering a few words of what was done to her. I ran to her barracks and after much encouragement, I persuaded her to go to the hospital. The poor woman was traumatized and ashamed at what her husband was going to think. As she was being examined, I reported the crime to the lieutenant's commanding officer, the captain in charge of him and my class of recruits.

Reporting our superior officer was akin to being a whistleblower but without the protection afforded under the usual reports of government waste, fraud, and abuse. However, I knew this call had to be made. After my notification, formal United States Army investigative procedures and protocols ensued. Things were precarious in the unit for a while. Tensions mounted as sides were drawn and assumptions made about guilt. In time, however, justice was served.

Upon the completion of my military training, I landed an investigator job at the Civilian Complaint Review Board (CCRB) for the city of New York. The CCRB evolved into a more independent agency in response to the tremendous public outcry over racially charged incidents and excessive abuse of police authority. CCRB investigators had subpoena authority and could recommend disciplinary measures in cases of substantiated police misconduct. I soon investigated cases involving public allegations against officers of the New York Police Department (NYPD).

There are subtle differences between an investigation of a civilian and that of a police officer brought to the CCRB. When a member of the public is interviewed/investigated, legal representation is typically not on hand. Officers were afforded guidance and presence of the Police Benevolent Association (PBA) representative during all officer interviews. Unlike the public, officers under investigation were permitted to review the complaint and discuss it with his/her PBA representative prior to the interview. For very good reasons, police officers under investigation who were about to be interviewed typically entered the interview rooms filled with tension, apprehension, and hostility.

My tactics were rather simple, yet many investigators could not master them. I always treated the officer and their PBA representatives with the respect they deserved, regardless of the accusations against them. The key to most human interactions is authenticity. I was always genuine in both civility and in expressing my anger when dealing with law enforcement professionals or the career criminal. Contrived emotion will always be sniffed out immediately.

I began by putting the police officers who were to be interviewed at ease. Their walls seemed to drop just enough to allow me a peek into their true selves. I would gently ask a question, careful not to offend or alarm, only to come back to it later several times. This typically resulted in the person becoming confused and disoriented as to what they had said. When inconsistencies arose or their answers didn't make sense, I would politely ask for forgiveness and continue probing for clarity, always working to keep them comfortable, careful to maintain the perceived balance of power.

At the CCRB, my interview techniques lulled the officers who had something to hide into a false sense of comfort. With my systematic, yet disarming line of attack, the guilty parties at some point would talk off script, often saying more than what was previously advised by counsel, only to realize it was too late.

The tape recorder could not be missed. There it was, placed dead center on the table, between myself and them. It recorded every word, subtle innuendo, question, denial, and stall tactic, and it always captured the information, unfiltered and raw. I always left the interrogation rooms as I entered them, with a big smile. Sometimes my smile was wider depending on what was caught on tape.

I was not in the business of going after cops—I wanted to get to the truth. I also applied my interrogation and interview techniques to civilians whose sole motivation was to use the CCRB to defame an active and honest cop. I had a natural instinct for detecting these phonies and would put an end to their ill-thought-out scheme.

In one case, officers assigned to the NYPD plainclothes street crime unit were getting slammed with CCRB complaints. The two officers, Billy Dentrone and Erick Hendricks, were some of the most dynamic, sincere, and reliable cops I had the pleasure of meeting. After interviewing these two dedicated public servants, separately of course, I determined they were honorable men who were truly trying to fight crime and protect the public. I pursued every opportunity to collect the information and evidence needed to prove the case filed against them was simply retribution from the criminal whom they had previously arrested.

To prove the officers' innocence, I had a major problem to overcome. I needed copies of the officers' memo book entries and other pertinent documents that the PBA representative advised them to, under no circumstances, provide me. This was standard procedure. Usually, this PBA practice made absolute sense. The PBA representative knew that by excluding the written information from the formal CCRB investigation, he would generally protect the officers from potential inconsistencies written in their daily log. Thus, by playing it safe and denying such requests, the PBA did, in fact, make it more difficult to prove their clients' guilt. However, they also made it more unlikely the officers' innocence would be demonstrated.

My sole intention was to do the right thing by them, namely, clearing their good names. In short, they agreed and provided me their daily log books against the advice of the PBA. I remain grateful to these men for taking a huge leap of faith and placing their trust in me, a young man and novice investigator. In return, I delivered exactly what I promised. I used their own written entries to help prove their innocence.

During a two-week Army Reserve assignment in Augsburg, Germany, I remember an encounter as if it were yesterday. A warrant officer by the name of Edward Mangano, an absolutely wonderful man, took me under his wing.

On day one, he called out to me, "Hey butter bar," a term loosely used for brand new second lieutenants. "You need to become a cop. I've got a hook at the Bronx District Attorney's Office, and they have a dedicated Detective Investigative squad that reports directly to the district attorney and conducts investigations. You'll have to go to the police academy and complete the training, but after that, you'll go straight to working cases. A smart guy like you, with a college education, that is the way to go. Then you can take that experience and apply to the feds. We all know they pay better."

As a member of the DI Squad, I knew my mission and purpose very clearly. Despite the DI Squad's poor reputation among established law enforcement entities and confusion as to its mission, purpose, and jurisdiction, I was respected by my counterparts. It was clear to me that the path forward to becoming a mob buster would, in time, become a reality. But not even I could anticipate how imminent my big break would be.

I never played or bought into office politics. I simply worked hard all the time. I avoided social gatherings, happy hours, and the long, never-ending squad lunches. I viewed all of this as a waste of time, and I had none to waste. I wanted to go after the mob, and I wanted to do it now. Looking back, I wonder who I would be as a man and where I would be in my professional life had I experienced a different upbringing. I, like my father, am a no-bullshit kind of man. Antonio Perrotta believed in a simple life but had a solid understanding that dedication to work and family were essential and nonnegotiable. Without the firm hand of my father while growing up as a tough kid, my destiny could have turned out like so many kids from my neighborhood…involved in a life of crime and dead ends—a life completely opposite from the one I chose and pursued.

In my favor were youth, exuberance, and success in developing confidential informants, locating witnesses, and closing cases. I developed a reputation for doing good quality work despite occasionally pissing off people who saw my aggressive work ethic as a threat.

My life changed forever the day I was summoned into the chief's office. In that meeting the chief of the Bronx District Attorney Detective Investigator Squad said to me, "We have a case, kid; lots of issues up there in White Plains, but, uh, we have a joint case with them, and it is a serious Mafia case." I was insanely thrilled and honored.

It was my second month on the job, and here I was, walking into my boss's boss's boss's office, wearing my Beretta 9 mm gun snug in my new shoulder rig just like I had imagined as a youth. And just like that, I was told to report to the New York State Organized Crime Task Force (OCTF) headquarters in White Plains, New York, within the week. I closed out all my remaining cases, cleared my makeshift desk, and enthusiastically left for White Plains, ready to begin the career I had always envisioned.

I later learned that the chief had previously assigned other DIs to White Plains to work the same joint case. Many of these veterans were all dismissed from OCTF for poor performance and incompetence. And those still assigned were in jeopardy of getting fired by the senior management running the case. So, the chief, who had no seasoned agents to activate, reluctantly assigned me to the case.

The assistant district attorney in charge of the case was Vincent Heintz, a tough prosecutor for the Bronx District Attorney's Office. The lead investigator from OCTF, Echo Gaudioso, was a retired NYPD sergeant and mentor to me. These men impressed me as no-nonsense professionals. And to this day, I respect them immensely.

I worked feverishly on a case that had been launched a few years prior. I put long days and nights into this case, mulling over case files and reviewing evidentiary items, learning and looking for clues. I was now engaged in my temporary assignment at the OCTF. I laid the groundwork to what would eventually become the biggest case of my career, the case against the Gambino crime family.

# 5　A Brief History: The Gambino Crime Family

I was about to embark on a journey fraught with risk. It was an obsession that totally consumed me. It occupied all of my waking hours and bit into what little sleep I managed to get. It slowly enveloped me and helped shape all my actions, thoughts, and relationships. It required full commitment and demanded all my energy. I had no time to engage in the typical fun someone my age would pursue. My marriage also fell victim. It failed, and we divorced only a few years after saying "I do." I sacrificed a great deal investigating the Gambino organized crime family. But I would do it all over again!

My family and friends lived in the area where I began to probe and poke at this big tiger. The Mafia had its grip on many facets of daily life for a New Yorker. The organized crime syndicate maintained a prominent, felonious element in the construction and trash hauling business, gambling, loan sharking, and narcotic dealings.

The Gambino family rose to the top of the Mafia food chain with the 1957 assassination of mob boss Albert Anastasia. He was murdered while sitting in a barber chair at the Park Sheraton Hotel in Manhattan. It was widely believed that Carlo Bambino, the underboss to Anastasia, had a hand in orchestrating the "hit" in a power move intended to take over the "family."

Prior to the 1957 assassination of Albert Anastasia, the Gambino crime family was one of five founding families in New York after the Castellammarese War that ended in 1931. The Gambinos occupied a minor role in the organized crime world during the next 25 years or so. However, during his reign, Anastasia was both ambitious and a force with which to be reckoned. Albert Anastasia was the most prominent member of the criminal organization. His penchant for violence and ruthlessness helped him rise in the ranks until he became the operating head of the underworld's enforcement arm, known as "Murder, Inc."

Although the group was dismantled by law enforcement in the late 1940s, Anastasia remained powerful within the organization and eventually took over the family in 1951 after, allegedly, murdering the family's founder, Vincent Mangano. The common theme here is the succession plan begins and ends with murder.

Carlo Gambino, a visionary, partnered with Meyer Lansky to take control of gambling interests in Cuba. This collaboration occurred prior to the military dictatorship of Fidel Castro. Under Carlo's leadership, the Gambinos gained fortune and power. In 1976, before his imminent death, Carlo Gambino appointed his brother-in-law Paul Castellano as boss of the family. This act rankled a brash, up-and-coming caporegime (captain or capo), a powerful and lofty position in the mob: John Gotti, later known as "Teflon Don" for his ability to elude federal conviction. Like Carlo Gambino, John Gotti used violence to achieve his goals and eventually orchestrated Castellano's murder in 1985 outside the infamous Sparks Steak House in Manhattan.

Teflon Don's downfall came in 1992, when his underboss, Salvatore "Sammy the Bull" Gravano, decided to cooperate with the FBI. Gravano's inside knowledge and secure position within the inner circle of the Mafia, coupled with his desire to save his own skin, led him to become a cooperating witness in the case against his former friend and boss, John Gotti.

Gravano's collaboration with the Department of Justice brought down Gotti, along with most of the top members of the Gambino family. With John Gotti behind bars where he eventually died of cancer, it was widely believed that Frank Cali took over as the head of the Gambino crime family. However, by 1995 the Gambino family was hemorrhaging.

The organization was riddled with arrests and numerous informants among its ranks. After what seemed like an eternity on the defensive, law enforcement was on firmer footing and finally making a dent in the criminal networks. The OCTF even had a case on Gregory "Greg" DePalma, a soldier in the Gambino family who had achieved infamy.

A quarter century earlier, in the mid-1970s, DePalma had befriended numerous A-list celebrities who frequented his newly built nightspot, the Westchester Premier Theatre in Tarrytown, New York. Among his new companions were Liza Minelli, Dean Martin, Willie Mays, and other famous people, including DePalma's most renowned friend: legendary singer and American icon Frank Sinatra.

As soon as the theatre opened its doors, DePalma began looting its cash and other assets. However, one year later, in 1978, DePalma was indicted on state charges stemming from the theatre's financial collapse. DePalma pleaded guilty to bankruptcy fraud. Ironically, the evidence that helped the prosecution's case was a picture of DePalma with Sinatra. DePalma was sentenced to 4 years in prison.

After serving his sentence, Greg DePalma was still a soldier in the Gambino crime family hierarchy. In the late 1990s DePalma was promoted to caporegime in the mob.

* * *

I worked at what was known as "the Plant," where the eavesdropping equipment used in the investigation was housed. Team members and I listened to intercepts, which were law enforcement recordings of conversations by Mafia associates.

One of the "bugs" was installed at the home of Gambino soldier, Greg DePalma in Scarsdale, New York. Also living with Greg was his wife Terry and one of his sons, Gambino mob soldier, Craig DePalma. In one critical conversation, Greg DePalma whispered to Mario Antonicelli about an issue with one of the rackets and discussed how to approach Louie Ricco. Upon hearing this, I said to my partner, "Hey, I'm going to do a drive-by at the DePalma residence." In no time, I ran out, jumped into my unmarked police vehicle, and within minutes arrived at the DePalma residence, just in time to take down the license plate number, make, and model of the visiting mobster's vehicle right before he pulled away. This physical surveillance of the gangster's whereabouts complemented what was heard on the wiretaps. This proof left little to the skeptical mind that the person heard was the same person exiting the residence. A physical description confirmed the vehicle, which was driven by Antonicelli, and later played a major role in the investigation.

I quickly learned that the extra steps I took almost floored the detective investigative sergeant. My pace, my urgency, my insistence on pushing the case forward completely caught him off guard. Almost immediately, the message became clear, "Hey slow down." That message didn't stop with him.

Soon enough, other supervisors joined the chorus, encouraging me in subtle and not so subtle ways to ease up, to take my time, to not be so quick. "Why rush?," they'd say. "Don't you want to enjoy the benefits that come with an assignment like this?" The detective investigator sergeant loved his take-home car. He loved leaving early. He loved the overtime.

As I listened to him, I realized the mission was not his priority. Benefits? I remember thinking, what the fuck is this clown talking about? I wasn't there for perks. I wasn't there to stretch a case out like taffy just to pad hours or keep a vehicle in the driveway. I was there to work, to move fast, collect evidence, and close cases. The idea that we shouldn't rush evidence collection so the overtime and take-home cars would last longer didn't just confuse me. It pissed me off. Did that even make sense? How had the mission become secondary to self-indulgence? I tried to process the reality, asking a question that kept echoing in my head: How the hell is this really happening to me?

That was my first real glimpse into the other mission, the one no one talked about out loud, but everyone seemed to understand. The investigation was initiated by the Bronx District Attorney's office after the New York State Senate referred information concerning allegations of corruption within the professional boxing world. Central to those concerns was Lenny Minuto, whose influence in the sport was widely rumored to extend into organized crime circles. Soon after, the Bronx DA Detective Investigative Squad forged a joint partnership with the OCTF.

Prior to my assignment to this case, the task force had dropped one of the wiretaps assigned to Craig (Greg's son) DePalma's cell phone. The task force incorrectly determined that the cell phone had minimal criminal value to the investigation and that Craig was not really involved in the day-to-day criminal activities of the Gambino crime family.

Upon my arrival to the case, I re-examined the evidence collected. Since growing up with wise guys in my father's deli, I was particularly astute to the nuances and eccentricities of their dialect. Soon after reviewing the transcripts, I realized that a great deal of information shared on Craig DePalma's cell phone did, in fact, have tremendous investigative value. Not only was this information significant but John Gotti Junior had also called that very cell phone. Upon further review of the audiocassettes, a conversation wherein Gotti Junior personally directed Craig DePalma to meet him was also intercepted.

I had collected so much evidentiary material that it was only natural for Vince and Echo to attest to the integrity of the investigation thus far and request the eavesdropping extension, which drove the case forward. Things would be serious from here on out. We were now targeting the head of the Gambino crime family: John Gotti Junior.

One night, a few minutes into a stakeout with Echo, we heard a loud crash. We looked out the windshield and saw the front of a vehicle horrifically wrapped around the steel pillar that supported a subway platform. I was the first to get to the crash site and find a young man and his mother inside the wreckage, obviously dead. We did not have a chance to attempt lifesaving techniques. They died upon impact. With the two bodies halfway out of the vehicle and blood everywhere, the planned surveillance on Greg DePalma was aborted.

I stood there feeling powerless when a young couple shouted my name. I looked up. Two students whom I knew from my college days coincidentally walked by as I apprehended the drunk driver responsible for the accident. Both former alumni were smiling upon their initial recognition of me, but those expressions faded upon seeing the scene unfold. The "innocence" of life as a student in college, at the moment we looked at each other, had vanished. As I handed the stumbling drunk over to the uniformed members of service that responded to the scene, clearly our new roles had been defined, and there was no turning back.

As soon as I reported to the OCTF, I was granted my first assignment: conduct surveillance on Greg DePalma and cover his impending meeting. Echo approached me with some matter-of-fact advice: "Look, when you follow these guys, don't be too aggressive and give them distance." At first take, I thought Echo's guidance made no sense and wondered why he did not offer more specific and helpful advice. I learned soon enough that, however succinct, no truer words have been said about the do's and don'ts of conducting surveillance.

My partner Vinney and I gathered our equipment, jumped into a surveillance vehicle, and were off with no training other than a 10-second sound bite from Echo. Despite our ill-prepared initiation, I could not help but smile. My childhood dream was actually about to be realized. I would soon surveil a high-target Mafia figure.

As the designated driver of the mission, I drove on the local streets of Yonkers, careful to appear relaxed, cool, and not the excited rookie I really was. The target vehicle sped up and slowed down intermittently. What was happening? I clearly saw Greg DePalma in the passenger seat look back at us—at me! How could this be? I was keeping my distance while maintaining a visual on them, trying to be as inconspicuous as possible. Yet, they easily shook our tail. These mobsters had years of experience being surveilled by police, and devised successful countermeasures, especially when important meetings were being held. I quickly learned that these were serious people, and if I was to be successful, I needed to treat them as such. To do otherwise would be foolish and costly.

We returned to the Plant with my tail between my legs, my pride diminished, and overcome with sadness. Echo found my demeanor amusing. Vinney began to contare, or "sing" in Italian, which means providing every bullshit excuse. I looked at Echo without hesitation and said, "Yeah. We got burned."

Echo could not help but smile. He knew we tried, and that was all he was looking for. "Look," he said. "Don't worry. This happens, and sometimes when you think you're getting burned, in reality, you're not." I simply shook my head in disgust with myself.

At the end of my shift, I went to the nearest bookstore and bought every true crime book about the Gambino crime family. In time, I deciphered seemingly innocuous references and comments and extracted invaluable material that helped provide investigative leads.

I surveilled several pagers (an electronic device that receives and sends basic messages, like a phone number—a staple in the 1990s) and listened to surveillance tapes day in and day out and learned their language, their jokes, and drew meaning to words and topics that others would find unrelated. I helped Linda, the only one assigned to transcribe the intercepted communications. Transcription was a tedious job but extremely helpful in adding to my overall knowledge and investigative strategy. As the summer ended, and with less than 6 months on the job, I steadily gained confidence in my abilities, and our clandestine operation proceeded like a well-oiled machine.

One afternoon, I had intercepted an unknown meeting off of Craig DePalma's cell phone. Since the transcripts to Craig's cell phone were virtually all relistened to by me, I was very familiar with the voices of those that called Craig. I immediately recognized the voice on the other end; it was John Gotti Junior, who was calling Craig DePalma. The incoming number was associated with JAG Construction. Soon after the call, Vince, Echo, and Linda as well as several other members of the task force verified that the voice belonged to John A. Gotti.

I was now able to report to my supervisors and the United States Attorney's Office that Junior was calling Craig. The cell phone's significance to the case grew exponentially. The cryptic conversations between Junior and Craig DePalma, who were obviously attempting to evade law enforcement, now demanded closer scrutiny. In support of my efforts, Echo said, "Sometimes all that is needed is taking an extra step or two, with an urgent sense of curiosity to give cases the acceleration needed so progress can begin." Before Echo could say another word, a beeping sound from our pager interrupted us. It was the Plant. I immediately dug into my pocket, retrieved loose change, and found the nearest pay phone to call the Plant. I was told that Craig had just been summoned and needs to meet "him" at Liberty Avenue in Queens. I repeated the message to Echo as I was hearing it. Echo and I looked at each other without a word and high-tailed it to Queens, New York.

The 32-mile distance under normal traffic conditions took about 45 minutes. But we had to get there before Craig did. The ride was a blur. I pushed the car beyond 100 mph, disregarding all sensibility for safety. I was determined to pass Craig and arrive on scene before the onset of the meeting. The Hutchinson River Parkway, with all its curves and nuances, seemed distorted with the mixture of sounds and colors of cars we passed. It was hypnotic, and we were running hot and silent. Echo was strapped to his seat, clutching the passenger door with his right hand while his left held the glove compartment. He braced himself for the inevitable impact and kept saying that he didn't know what was more dangerous—the Gambino family or my driving!

Pulling off the Van Wyck Expressway, Echo spotted Craig's car, a silver Chevy Blazer. This time, I kept my distance. I was not going to get burned on this one, not again. The Blazer pulled alongside a black Oldsmobile. Sharing binoculars, Echo and I saw Craig talking to two men. Unbelievably, on the passenger side of the Oldsmobile, we identified John Gotti Junior. This established the link between Craig DePalma and the Gambino crime boss. This vital connection enabled us to obtain judicial approval for the placement of wiretaps on Gotti's phones and bugs in his offices.

After 2 hours of surveillance, Echo determined it best to vacate the scene before getting noticed. Shortly after driving away, we were followed. Our "tail" was a dark Suburban with three men inside. Echo quickly noted the license plate number, which through further research revealed that the car was registered to Carmine Agnello's junkyard business. Agnello was Gotti Junior's brother-in-law and also a suspected member of the Gambino crime family.

The Suburban positioned along my right side at a red light. Their car window opened, and one of the men asked, "How's it going?" Their hands were hidden; their eyes trained on us. At that moment, I expected to see them pull out a shotgun. That's when Echo reached into the glove compartment and took out our police parking credential. He flashed it and said, "We're good guys, just working." The Suburban quickly drove away.

Despite the near altercation with the mobsters, Echo and I were euphoric at the success. With the OCTF intercepting Gotti's phone call summoning Craig to meet in an abandoned warehouse, we were there to witness and record every incriminating moment of it. We were closing in and moving up the food chain of the Gambino hierarchy.

In a state of fanatical obsession, I sat at my desk before, during, and after my shift at the Plant listening to every intercepted word and pondering over the written transcripts. I easily identified every voice that was transmitted over our sanctioned listening devices. My knowledge of the players, both the primary and secondary members, became a permanent part of my memory.

We executed a search warrant at Greg and Craig DePalma's shared residence, expecting that after law enforcement left, invaluable and revealing conversations among the suspects would ensue. We synchronized our search warrants at various mob locations to increase our chances of gleaning important information. We referred to this technique as "tickling the bug." While I sat at the Plant, I listened to telephone conversations. A telltale sign that known members of the crime family were about to discuss something noteworthy was that the volume on the TV would abruptly rise.

This time I heard Greg DePalma in a fit of rage, yelling at his wife. Echo and I were curious as to the cause of his anger and endless use of profanity. We listened and learned that after the execution of an earlier search warrant at his home, DePalma was furious because the OCTF investigators found and seized his stash of marijuana, used for his personal enjoyment. In between his barrage of insults at his wife and "those fucking scumbag cops," DePalma paused and whispered his relief that the "money hidden in the rafters" was never uncovered during the search.

After obtaining the required legal approvals, we returned to DePalma's home and recovered more than $250,000. In subsequent surveillance, we heard DePalma in the midst of yet another verbal tirade filled with fury and insults to his wife of 30 years. "You're a rat…a dirty, gutter rat. You're nuttin' but a dirty gutter rat." It was as sad as it was comical.

The case moved along nicely. As I learned more about our targets and became more experienced, upper management granted me more investigative flexibility and responsibilities. Echo and Vince were pleased with my performance. Once again, the opportunity presented itself for me to push the investigative envelope. Filled with confidence and a sense of purpose, I directed my efforts toward a new approach not previously undertaken at the OCTF.

I requested a court order to clone the pager of DePalma's son, Craig DePalma. Thus, I would receive notification in real time whenever Craig received a page. Although the pager messages were cryptic, I discovered a pattern. Over several weeks of analysis, I noticed the receipt of a page sent only on Wednesdays. The phone toll records also confirmed a pattern of numbers, in no discernable sequence. For example, a page had the following numbers: 101900 or 101930.

While reading yet another true crime book on the Gambino family during my shift at the Plant, a breakthrough occurred. I read a line that described the Bergin Hunt and Fish Club. There it was, the physical address of this storied hangout and headquarters made infamous by the legendary mob boss John J. Gotti Sr., also known as the "Dapper Don." The club was located at 98-04 101$^{st}$ Avenue in Ozone Park. At the sight of this "101" sequence, I had an epiphany. Could it be possible that Craig was being summoned to 101st Street and the numbers that followed on the page be the time to report? It made sense. 101900—could mean to meet at the location at 9 p.m. The obvious was hidden in plain sight.

Despite the numerous surveillances conducted on the Bergin Hunt and Fish Club by various law enforcement agencies, and that it was a confirmed Mafia joint, it remained the place where mob boss John Gotti Junior held court. I ran my theory by Echo and Vince. They were amazed and agreed that we should surveil the club the next time the pager indicated such a meeting. Like clockwork, the following Wednesday, the pager received the code: 101900. At the expected meeting time and location, our team was in position to surveil the club. We, however, were in a white Ford Pinto, which called too much attention to itself. But there was no time to object. Things were moving fast with no time to debate the details, regardless of the danger.

The OCTF team positioned itself strategically to cover every direction in and out of the club. Many cars in the area moved up and down the street and people loitered on the sidewalks. Approximately 30 minutes before the onset of the meeting, two hulking henchmen stepped out of the club. One of them carried a baseball bat as they canvassed the area and challenged anyone nearby in or out of a vehicle. One by one, the henchmen directed the surveillance vehicles to leave. Rather than face an altercation, my OCTF partners left the scene, choosing to break the surveillance and fight another day.

As the two mobsters approached our vehicle, I grabbed my partner, Roger, by his head and placed it firmly on my lap. "What the fuck are you—," he started to say, but I told him to shut up and keep his head down. From a distance it looked like I, the driver, was getting sexually gratified. As I acted out faux euphoria, I kept one eye on the two approaching thugs and a hand on my .38 snub-nosed revolver. The men came within 20 feet of our car, looked at each other, turned, and walked away.

Roger and I collected substantial evidence as we witnessed key players showing up at the club. With the path now clearly defined and the hunt underway, we were moving up the organized crime food chain. They had no idea what was about to happen. I knew it was only a matter of time before I would capture our prey. In the short term, however, I had a lot of explaining to do with my surveillance partner and friend Roger.

## 6  Check Forgery Squad

As I concluded my time with OCTF, my last highly influential contribution was swearing to the December 1995 state affidavit. This groundbreaking investigative technique authorized the Interception Team to expand the number of targets that could be surveilled by wiretap, including the head of the Gambino crime family—John Gotti Junior.

In 1996, after another 6 months between two training academies—the Federal Law Enforcement Training Academy in Georgia and the United States Secret Service Academy in Maryland—I was ready to start my career as a newly commissioned Secret Service agent.

The day I swore an oath to defend the American public and the United States Constitution as a Secret Service agent was, and remains, one of the proudest moments of my life.

I reported to 7 World Trade Center, the home of the respected New York Field Office. The agents reporting there varied in professional background. Some were police, detectives, and lawyers in previous careers. To break in the new agents, we were assigned to the Check Forgery Squad.

New agents such as myself learned the basics of investigations. Most of the check cases involved forgeries, such as altered checks to make the original dollar amount higher; a fake payee signature; or a false claim of theft by the check's recipient in the hopes of receiving a replacement check and cashing both the original and replacement checks to double their monthly Social Security, disability, or tax refund checks.

The check squad was the place to indoctrinate new recruits on the New York approach to solving check-related crimes by the book. Another check agent and I went to Brooklyn to "investigate" a check case, which meant obtaining as much information as possible to close the case. We needed to do this before we began our 3-week protection detail for President Clinton's 1996 re-election campaign.

We drove to Brooklyn in an old, beat-up Crown Victoria, which was a typical police-driven vehicle well known among criminals. Moreover, due to a new dress code, my partner and I had to wear business suits. We stood out and were overheated in the suits. When we arrived at the target residence located in the projects, my partner expressed his reluctance to park next to where the subject lived out of fear of our car getting vandalized by the adults loitering in the area. I insisted he park directly in front of our subject's home because the suits were broiling us and we didn't have a working air conditioner in the Crown Vic. I told him that I could give a rat's ass if they set the car on fire; it would be a blessing.

After my partner parked, I saw a man who seemed down on his luck, leaning against a wall. I called him over. At first, he refused because he knew we were law enforcement due to our dress code and vehicle make and model. But I convinced him to approach us, and I said to him, "Listen, all is good; no worries. See this car?" He replied, "Yeah, I see it…" "Okay, this car belongs to my friend here. He loves this car; lost his virginity in this car." The guy laughed. I continued, "Do me a favor. I have a job for you… You need a job?" "Yeah, sure," he grunted. "Okay, if I give you some money, you watch my friend's car. Make sure your boys don't fuck with it." "Yeah, I can do that," he said, now really interested.

I told my partner to give him some money. He looked at me as if to say, "I don't want to give him my money." I said, "You cheap fuck. Pay my guy here so he can watch the car or you process the paperwork explaining why you drove to the Brooklyn projects with a Crown Vic and returned with only a steering wheel." My partner gave up a $20 bill, and I promised the guy if he did a good job, I'd have another twenty for him.

We entered one of the buildings, located the target apartment, and knocked. "Who's there?" we heard. "The police!" I said in a loud, authoritative voice. She screamed back in a strong Jamaican accent, "I ain't call no police." I replied, "Do you want your check refund or not?"

The door opened with the woman smiling ear to ear. She was very overweight and wearing a housedress that did a poor job of covering her up. We thought we had seen enough overexposure. But as the interview proceeded, we were about to see a hell of a lot more.

She led us in. The apartment was disgusting. To no surprise, the place was infested with cockroaches. With her consent, we conducted a quick safety check of the premises to ensure there were no hidden dangers. Then we sat at a round table in the kitchen and asked her to explain what happened to her refund check. We listened as she attempted to explain how her check must have been stolen from the broken mailbox in the building's lobby. She elaborated that she thought she knew the group of men who stole her check. Employing all the techniques we learned in Secret Service school, we nodded our heads, listened, and appeared non-judgmental. My partner and I agreed with her and told her that we have been working hard on such a crime syndicate in the area, a bullshit story to keep her unsuspecting that we were on to her.

We asked her, "as a matter of protocol," to sign her name on government-issued handwriting sample cards. We had her sign her name on about 100 cards during our session with her. With her first 20 signatures, it was apparent she was trying to conceal her actual signature, which we would compare to the back of the returned "stolen" check. We told her we would use these samples to convince our boss she was not guilty. We told her that we believed she was a good and honest woman who would NEVER commit fraud against the United States government and file a false claim, would she? "No mon," she kept saying.

As she continued to provide writing samples of her signature, she complained that her hand hurt and asked if she could stop. "No, just a few more to go. You know government paperwork and all." After about 15 monotonous minutes of her signing her name over and over, her best efforts to conceal her actual signature failed.

We were by no means handwriting experts, but it only took a layman to instantly recognize her signature samples #50 through #100 closely matched the back of the supposedly "stolen" Treasury check. At this point, we had her. We told her that she would be charged to the fullest extent of federal law for committing such a horrible crime, when in fact the United States Attorney's Office would never have even accepted the case for criminal prosecution due to the low dollar amount of the actual check. But what the hell! She did not need to know that. We had a case to close and city traffic to get through to process the paperwork for this "dog," a case deemed a waste of time.

This woman cried hysterically, yelled, and appeared to be close to fainting or having a heart attack. As already noted, she was a BIG woman, and neither my partner nor I wanted to face having to initiate mouth-to-mouth resuscitation on her should she drop to the kitchen floor.

Realizing that we may have pushed too far with the empty threats of facing hard time in a federal prison, we offered her an out. "Just give us a good reason, you know, so we can tell our boss why you did this… Perhaps you were mistaken and confused when you signed the claim of a stolen check?"

"Yeah, you right, mon," she said. "You know I was in a car accident, had me an operation and high blood pressure…You know me were confused on the month, you know…Maybe I did get that check…Now me think about it."

"Yes, that's what happened," I said. But just as we were at a point of conclusion, my partner felt he had to press her more and call out her BS. He asked her to essentially provide proof of her medical procedure she just claimed to have undergone.

"You know…me go under the knife, look at me scar," she said desperately trying to back up her story, even though evidence of any operation was not apparent. "Look at me scar, mister," she said as she grabbed her left breast and whipped out the biggest boob I have ever seen. It was so big that it almost knocked over the handwriting samples as she laid it out on the table. Even the roaches scattered at the sight of it. She insisted there was a scar under her breast. My partner looked away from her exposed nudity, clearly mortified. She put herself back into her dress and insisted her made-up car accident caused her confusion about receiving, signing, and cashing the subject check.

Just to bust my partner's balls, I asked her to pull "it" out again so "we" could get a better look at her scar

56

in case we had to testify in court. She whipped out her floppy boob again as my partner quickly gathered all the paperwork and hurried to the door, thanking her for her time. I was laughing my ass off.

By the time I completed the U.S. Army training, the Rockland Policy Academy, and the Secret Service training, I was able to channel my energy exclusively toward catching criminals. I loved the hunt and reveled in unraveling the unknown pieces that are part of any investigation. This activity, both mentally and physically demanding, kept me focused. I found my calling.

During this time of intense investigative activity and in the years following, I was all-consumed and fulfilled when on a mission. Early on, it was Echo who looked at me with surprise and said that I had a gift. At first, I didn't understand what he meant, but with time, I realized his point. I consistently predicted what would happen in a particular setting or case, then would see it play out as I had envisioned. I was becoming a damn good investigator. Hunches would turn into solid investigative leads. Very soon, the office and the agency would learn of my abilities and my commitment to the job and to the victims of crime.

## 7    Bank Fraud Squad

A fellow agent on the tenth floor rang my desk phone looking to punt a potential case that had been recently assigned to the Bank Fraud Squad. She claimed she was too busy to handle the complaint. This agent in the Bank Fraud Squad was right out of the academy, so I documented the general details from her about the case and took it over. I contacted the complainant, John, the head of security of a midtown Manhattan firm.

John explained the situation: an employee who worked in one of the tenant offices at the building had his personal mail stolen. He apparently did not receive his federal tax refund check, which was deposited into an account not belonging to the victim. I called the United States Postal Inspection Service and confirmed that the check had been delivered 4 days prior. All incoming mail, including the check in question, was recorded as received at the mailroom.

Then I requested the schedule and the employee names of those who worked in the mailroom at the time the check was delivered to the mailroom. John responded, "Everyone, except one, an employee who was out on medical leave and did not report to work due to a foot injury sustained prior to this issue of the stolen check." I instructed John to hold everyone in the mailroom, not to let them go home. "Tell them this is a national security issue and that the Secret Service is on the way to question everyone." I was on my way...

One piece of information John did not get from the victim proved essential in the investigation. John obtained this extra piece of information from an unrelated investigation by the FBI-NYPD Joint Robbery Task Force. They were investigating a woman, Rachelle Commodore, who was a teller at the European American Bank. This bank had been held up at gunpoint on three separate occasions. Rachelle's boyfriend, Adrian Carne, my soon-to-be subject, worked in the mailroom at the security firm. I informed John that I wanted to interview Adrian last.

I interviewed each employee one at a time in an empty mailroom office. I kept each of them for about 30 minutes, asking all sorts of questions that had nothing to do with the real reason I was there. But I was setting the stage of my play. Once I got to Adrian, the subject who I believed stole the check, my line of questioning changed.

When Adrian, a young, thin, tall male, entered the room, I introduced myself: "My name is Nino Perrotta. I'm a Special Agent with the United States Secret

Service. Do you know why I am here?" He responded, "Yeah, uh, somebody threatened the president."

I corrected him with my creative explanation. "No, no, no…That's what I told your friends in order to protect you. You see, the Secret Service has a lot of satellites, and we are constantly watching people who may be of interest to us. We also protect the money and all federal checks from getting compromised, or in this case, stolen. Would you like me to show you at my office the video we collected from our satellites of you taking a check last week from this mailroom in the amount of $17,000?" Instantly Adrian's head tilted downward, an all-too-common sign that he was ready to cooperate.

I told Adrian, "You know we can fix this issue, but I will need you to cooperate with me." A bit confused and afraid of the consequences, Adrian ultimately told me how his girlfriend at the bank was the one who forced him to do it, and that they have a baby together, and he loves her. I responded, "Listen to me; show me you want this behind you. You make a call to her and all you need to say is that you have another check for her." He agreed, and from the office with my little black bag of technical devices, he made the recorded call to Rachelle.

She didn't bite all the way, but she did agree to discuss the check once he came home. I successfully met a suspect and got him to confess to stealing the check, sign a confession statement, and implicate his girlfriend.

As I processed the paperwork from my office, I received a call from Tom Buda, a detective with the NYPD. All was fine with the conversation until he said he was with the FBI Joint Robbery Task Force. *The FBI? What do they want?* I thought. After learning the outcome of my case from John, head of Security, Detective Tom Buda shared facts of an unsolved bank robbery he was working on and how their main subject was Adrian's girlfriend, Rachelle Commodore, a bank teller at the European American Bank.

Buda and his partner, Walter Carroll—a brilliant FBI Special Agent—were investigating suspicious circumstances of three armed bank robberies at the same branch where Commodore had at one time worked. Buda and Carroll were increasingly frustrated since all their leads hit dead ends.

The Bank Robbery Task Force was formed in 1979 and its purpose was to investigate armed bank robberies in New York City and apprehend individuals committing these robberies. The unit operated in four boroughs: Manhattan, the Bronx, Brooklyn, and Queens. All cases handled by the task force were jointly investigated with a police detective and an FBI agent.

During 1980, the first full year of the task force's operation, armed bank robberies in the city dropped from 319 in the preceding year to 252.

Even though Buda and Carroll had Commodore as their primary suspect, they were unable to solve the armed bank robberies without her cooperation. She had responded to all questions with a frigid standard, "NO." Denial seemed to be deeply embedded in her veins.

My case against Adrian, who admitted to giving his girlfriend, Rachelle Commodore, the stolen check, breathed new life into the FBI-NYPD joint investigation. My case provided the hook into Commodore. Therefore, after Adrian's confession, I collected additional information that placed Commodore at the center of the stolen check case conspiracy.

The collected information was powerful and damning evidence. The stolen check had been deposited on or about December 1996 into a fictitious bank account at the European American Bank, the branch where Commodore worked and where all three robberies occurred.

Armed with this evidence, I knew exactly what to do and how to crack this cold case. I engaged Commodore almost daily, both in person and on the telephone. I was extremely careful not to press too hard, so as to gain her trust and confidence.

In the afternoon of February 10, 1997, I drove my unmarked police car to pick up Commodore at her residence. I made an important stop before arriving. I picked up three Italian subs: one for her; one for the female agent who was required to be present whenever transporting a female; and one for me. We ate them on the drive downtown to the New York Field Office at 7 World Trade Center.

As we approached the building, I radioed the Secret Service dispatcher, who notified building security to open their massive steel garage doors. I slowly pulled through. Commodore laughed the entire way down to my office and continued to make jokes and laugh during the booking process. She waived her Miranda rights by signing the appropriate forms. As we photographed and fingerprinted her, I made sure no one either offended her or treated her disrespectfully. In law enforcement, mostly due to frustration, agents often make disparaging remarks to "perps." I wanted to avoid that since the woman had gone through a great deal in her life, living in Harlem under very tough conditions. She was a single parent for the most part, and looking at some serious jail time. Also, the last thing I wanted was for her to feel that I was against her, which potentially could jeopardize her willingness to cooperate on the bank robbery case.

My gentle handling, kind gestures, and the Italian sandwiches worked in my favor. Just as we were about to take her to the Southern District of New York where the U.S. Marshal Service would take custody, Commodore gestured to me that she had something to tell me about the bank robberies. I took her into the interview room where she provided me the outline of her involvement and that of others.

With her and Adrian's statements and the evidence collected, we had enough to arrest and convict her. But her check case confession became the grease that finally loosened her lips. She began to talk.

Commodore's story began with a man she identified as Kiki and how she gave him the best times to enter the bank and initiate their scheme. She explained the steps on how they planned the robberies and how they argued over money and how, during one of the robberies, Kiki had waved a gun in her face. She was pissed at the time. And during the confession, she explained the act of waving a gun in her face was completely disrespectful. Notwithstanding all the drama from Commodore, we had the confessions, and we were now focused on identifying the other suspects.

Once Commodore confessed to her involvement, she made the pivot to becoming my informant. Then I turned my attention toward identifying the other bank robbers caught on bank surveillance. I reviewed phone toll records that my colleagues, Buda and Carroll, requested for the case. Toll records are voluminous lists of telephone calls, both incoming and outgoing, that are made from a particular phone within a billing cycle. Phone records are similar to a fingerprint left at a crime scene. Each phone user had their distinctive habits and patterns, and I looked for those patterns in this investigation.

In an effort to identify the other bank robbers and piece together their inner circle, I subpoenaed all the phone records during each month before and after all three armed robberies. I started with Commodore's landline at the bank and her cell phone in the hopes this research would produce a potential lead or even a suspect.

To quicken the pace of the investigation, I favored applying more pressure on the person with the most to lose, Commodore. Buda and Caroll both agreed. Although the phone records produced a very important lead, it was Rachelle Commodore who gave everyone the break they were looking for.

At a suspicious time, approximately minutes prior to one of the robberies, a call was made to Commodore's cell phone. It came from another bank not far from the European American Bank. With the surveillance photos assembled as part of the public awareness flyer circulated throughout New York City, Buda and I headed to this other nearby bank to seek out any potential leads. We were at the bank no more than 5 minutes asking general questions when an employee identified one person from the surveillance photos as a man who worked in the mailroom. The guy left the job a week prior to our visit. The bank robbers were career criminals, all young men with violent pasts. They were part of a Rastafarian crime group operating in Manhattan and Brooklyn.

Buda was dumbfounded by Commodore's level of cooperation with me. He finally asked her why she decided to cooperate with the investigation. She replied, "You guys were assholes, and Nino was so kind and gentle with me." With Commodore's cooperation, we were able to close the case and get the armed and dangerous culprits off the street… It was an honor.

The details of the case spread through the Secret Service field office. I was given an on-the-spot award for my achievements. Soon afterward, agents were asking me how I conducted my investigations. But I wasn't looking for adulation and being put on a pedestal. I was already busy working cases, looking for my next target, and was not interested in the fluff.

Some of the other agents felt compelled to brag about their number of arrests. Internally, I questioned them. It is not about the number of arrests made; it's all about the number of convictions. Therefore, an effective Secret Service agent works alongside the prosecutor and identifies a network, as opposed to a smash-and-grab case, which is more the local authority street crime approach. We, the Secret Service, should not be making minor arrests.

Our job was not street crime. So to hear some agents tell me how many arrests they made, basically for drug users or homeless folks stealing Treasury checks from a mailbox, was not impressive at all. We are the Secret Service, and although protecting the integrity of the mail system and federally issued checks is important, we needed to elevate ourselves and look at the bigger picture.

While working this high-profile bank robbery case, I simultaneously continued working on mob leads. Within months after the successful outcome of the Commodore/bank robbery case, I identified additional key Mafia targets and had obtained court orders (all related to a fraud scheme involving prepaid calling cards) through the prosecuting team for a series of new pen registers (a device that identifies routing, addressing, or signaling information of a wire transmission). It was clear I had begun to "shake" the Gambino crime family tree once again.

## 8  A Major Breakthrough

In the mid-1990s, the syndicate involved itself in the prepaid calling card business, and within a short period, wreaked havoc on the telecommunications industry. The syndicate was untouchable, and seeing that their success received no attention from law enforcement, they continued to loot the poor consumers and the wealthy telecommunications giants.

While newly assigned to the New York Field Office (7 World Trade Center) as a Special Agent, I worked almost every night at the White Plains, Southern District of New York office plodding through voluminous wiretap conversations until I couldn't keep my eyes open. While I listened to an intercepted conversation from 1996, suddenly, among the Mafiosos talking, the conversation turned to just two people. One of them was John Gotti Junior.

At the time, I was unaware of the enormous impact this particular intercepted conversation would have to an overall scheme. The original OCTF transcript had a great number of details missing and ultimately looked nothing like the product I produced after countless reviews and revisions. This is in no way a criticism of the work produced by others. My predecessors religiously cranked out these transcripts. But there was too much work on these types of cases and few to no resources to perfect the work product. Many of the intercepted conversations, particularly the ones that discussed fraud, had many gaps in the transcripts. Why? Unlike well-known traditional schemes where the investigator and transcriber are highly experienced, this unprecedented telecommunications fraud confounded the folks behind the bug. The lack of experience, coupled with understaffing, resulted in information missed and/or minimized during the intercept, and later on transcripts.

Prior to my investigative involvement, other agents had reviewed the evidence and incorrectly concluded that there was no case for fraud. By this time, I had re-transcribed about 300 to 400 intercepted wiretapped conversations. Conclusively, there was major fraud going on.

* * *

This tedious, labor-intensive procedure of listening to all the conversations from scratch allowed me to dissect every word recorded, and slowly I reconstructed the fraud scheme.

After repeatedly reading the newly revised transcript of the conversations, a phrase caught my attention. I kept replaying the same few seconds of the conversation where the word *bustin'* was said, with the hope to either confirm or deny what appeared to be a major discovery.

At one point as I slowly replayed Gotti's every word, I heard him say the word *bustin'*. Can this be true? Was Gotti informing Plomitallo that "his" intent with the phone card business was to bust it out?

To be clear, "bustin' out" is a Mafia colloquialism for intentionally imploding a business opportunity to exploit its assets and credit worthiness. An analogy would be if a man or woman intentionally married a partner for the sole purpose of taking their partner's assets, savings, and maxing out their credit cards until the partner goes bankrupt. Then, after a divorce, the fraudster marries another person and does the same thing over again. When the mob busts out a business, they take it over and exploit all opportunities to acquire its assets, including credit, until it goes bankrupt.

What was later an even more profound breakthrough was the fact that Gotti Junior, in that particular conversation, tied the conspiracy events between an earlier prepaid calling card fraud scheme to the one that took place later with his business and Denny McLain, the ex-pitcher for the Detroit Tigers.

A conspiracy to "bust out" the fraudulent prepaid calling card business that Gotti and the syndicate controlled was intercepted, and I found it!

Once I was confident of what was said, I immediately contacted Echo, who I woke up from a sound sleep. I then did the same to Vince Heintz and discussed the evidence I heard on the cassette tape. The next morning, a buzz was in the air. Everyone was excited, including the other attorneys from the Southern District of New York.

What I heard in that transcript was a conspiracy being plotted by the head of the Gambino crime family. John Gotti Junior, that May 28, 1996, had a conversation where he, for a brief moment, felt secure and explained to Plomitallo his intent to control an expanding prepaid calling card fraud scheme. That evening, he identified himself as the "master broker" who would control all the prepaid calling card companies. At the time, I wasn't sure how much influence the Gambinos had over this scheme. But after numerous interviews, strategic search warrants, and listening to every intercepted conversation that followed the May one, it was clear that they had complete control of the distribution of the prepaid calling card market.

Amazingly, the original wiretaps enabled by the December 1995 affidavit that I brokered in the judge's kitchen, ultimately captured various criminal enterprises, including the scheme behind the prepaid calling card fraud.

The May 28, 1996, conversation tied Gotti Junior to the Travel Card, which had committed major fraud. By spring of 1996, the Travel Card was activating approximately 20 million phone cards a month before it went bankrupt in late 1996.

To understand the issue and the reason why Gotti Junior was explaining his plan to have multiple companies up and running had to do with the eventual shutoff of service. The cards sold would eventually not work since the companies producing them had no intention of paying the carrier in full. The intercepted conversation captured Gotti Junior providing a solution to enable the fraud to continue after a prepaid calling card business went defunct. Gotti explained that having another card company ready to replace the one that no longer was in business would be the way to proceed. This would minimize attention and outside scrutiny.

* * *

By overwhelming the industry with subpoenas, conducting physical surveillance at unheard-of hours, using technology by cloning and intercepting pager communications, analyzing voluminous phone records that resulted in pen register requests, and my hunches, which at times seemed like witchcraft because so many of them uncovered truths of criminal activity, the case moved from a snail's pace to rocket speed.

Soon after the new fraud evidence was collected and analyzed, the Gambino crime family received its first official notification that a federal agency, not familiar to them, was knocking on their doorstep. On October 7, 1997, a Federal Search Warrant that Special Agent Nino Perrotta swore to, was executed at Nic O Dan Communications, located at 97-11 Sutphin Boulevard, Queens, New York. This was John A. Gotti Junior's prepaid calling card business, named after his two children.

Before we raided the place, we did our homework and knew that adjacent to Nic O Dan Communications was Carmine Agnello's business, Jamaica Auto Salvage / Agnello Auto Parts. Carmine was a complete nut job and one scary-looking mobster who at the time was married to Junior's sister, Victoria Gotti.

A hulking man at the entrance to Nic O Dan identified himself as Steve Dobies. I looked up at him and, without a word, showed him the search warrant. We had the NYPD major case squad there for backup if needed. Dobies stood at least 6'3" and commanded a lurking appearance. We told him to stand aside so that we could conduct our search. Dobies had a concerned look on his face and informed me that his boss, John Gotti Junior, was on the phone and wanted to speak to me, and that it was urgent.

I took the call on Dobies' phone, and "Junior" explained, in a very cordial manner, that there was absolutely no need for such an event. He said that if I had asked in advance, he would have been more than happy to cooperate and make copies of business files, and in the same breath, offered me and the search team some expresso and pastries. I smirked since I understood the friendly gesture but respectfully declined, thanked him, and handed the phone back to Dobies and went on with the search.

We found the intercepted cassette recordings provided to the defense team of the imprisoned John Gotti Senior. These recordings were intended for the defense team, which was tasked to the infamous FBI case where Sammy "The Bull" Gravano became a cooperating witness against the Gambinos.

When we got to Gotti Junior's office, we noticed several pictures and statues of Native Americans. We were informed later that Junior and his sister believed that the Gotti family, like the Native Americans, were hunted and persecuted, and thus they believed that they were "the last of the Mohicans."

In the end, we got what we were looking for then left. Until this time, the only interaction I'd had with Gotti Junior was on surveillance. At no other time did I speak with him, but despite the brief and innocuous exchange between us, the feeling was overwhelming. The fact that I spoke to my "target" was an absolute charge. I could feel my blood flowing through my body, but remained calm and focused, which made me ever so confident of my surroundings and purpose.

The search was important. It provided that the "conspiracy" conversation we heard in the car moved forward, and intent for fraud was established. The search warrant also produced interesting information: an unusual number of phone cards ordered for print, and thousands of labels with an 800 number followed by an activation PIN. Our forensics experts determined that the number of cards activated for use did not match the number of prepaid calling cards printed, and they did not correlate with the new 800 number/activation label. Therefore, the cards were never intended to work as advertised.

In addition to the prepaid calling cards, which were called Liberty Tel, we found a document on the secretary's computer. This document seemed to read like a diary that contained a history of events that involved the fraudulent prepaid calling card business, which incriminated several key individuals.

## 9　The Gambino Phone Card Scheme Explained

With the mob's traditional control of extortion and bid-rigging rackets weakened by years of relentless prosecutions, the New York region's Mafia crime families were switching to white-collar crimes. The mob focused on multimillion-dollar frauds in three lucrative businesses: health insurance, small Wall Street brokerage houses, and prepaid telephone cards.

The Gambinos profited tens of millions of dollars by selling fraudulent prepaid, long-distance calling cards. In the 1990s, people made international phone calls by using prepaid calling cards. With a payment of $5, $10, or $20, a calling card could be purchased from a retail outlet. The card provided a personal identification number (PIN) and a toll-free access number. To use the card, both the PIN and access numbers were keyed in on the telephone key pad to make a long-distance call for, supposedly, the amount of time the card advertised. The consumer dialed the long-distance number with the understanding that the prepayment was much cheaper than using normal long-distance carrier services.

The scam entailed advertising low international long-distance calling rates. But the rock-bottom rates were offered only because the mob was never going to pay their carrier for the services rendered. In addition, the mob provided fewer minutes of calling time than what the cards advertised, so many long-distance cards that advertised 20 minutes, shut off after a fraction of that time.

This scam in itself defrauded the most vulnerable in our society, hardworking immigrants mostly from Asia, South America, and Africa. These were the kind of folks that after working long, long shifts in the back of a restaurant would run to the nearest pay phone to hear the voice of their loved ones only to sadly be interrupted with a calling card that had only seconds of phone service rather than the advertised minutes.

These cards were supposed to benefit those less fortunate, but instead the fraudulent cards exploited them. To me this was especially insulting, and I would often hear from the victims who mailed me their complaint letters with their now defunct and worthless phone cards enclosed:

18/07/1996

Nagib C. (victim who purchased fraudulent phone card) wrote:

Did any of you try these Conetco prepaid cards, and if so, how is your experience with it? If not, be aware, indeed, I lost $40, but I hate for anybody else to lose any more money if it is a scam.

I used these cards for the past 2 years. And trust me, it was less than 79 cents a minute. The company is out of business. Why?

18/07/1996
This message is to share information with the rest of you. A month ago, I saw the ad for calls to Lebanon for $.79 a minute. I went ahead and bought two of them from Mr. El K., thinking that everything is legit. When I got the cards. I tried them and was kind of disappointed with the charges since it did not match with the time spent. For example, I talked for 10 minutes and got charged for 14 minutes. So like a sucker, I went ahead and paid for them since the total amount was not worth returning them and paid more postage on top of the whole thing. So I kept them to finish later. I had 31 minutes left. However, I have been trying to call their 800 number for the last month and was never able to get connected after that.

Mr. K answered:

Hello N,

First of all, I am just responsible for selling cards. I am not responsible for the timing and the rates and how to connect. The rate on the cards I sent you was 79c/min to Lebanon, and the timing is done by the computer and is the same as AT&T timing. I ask everybody to use the cards before they send me the money to make sure that I am not trying to rip them off, and I asked you to use the cards before you send me the money. All what I do is buying cards from wholesale and selling them within their pricing value. And I do not own or operate those companies. So if you have a problem with them, you can call their customer service and complain. Anyway, if you still have a card unopened, I will send you a refund.

Regards Serge EL-K

These communications pertain to the prepaid calling cards during the peak of the scam. All the letters I received had a common theme: the consumer had purchased phone cards that stopped working without warning and/or the cards cheated them out of phone time. The mob also shut off phone cards while they were in use, forcing the consumer to reconnect, which automatically charged a $1 fee to the user. This was called a "bong" charge. These premature card stoppages were possible with the Mafia's full control of switches and fraudulent IPOs. It was nearly an undetectable scheme.

Soon those involved in selling the prepaid calling cards were reaching out to me. I had more cooperating witnesses on this case than on all other cases combined.

Some of these resellers were real characters, especially the ones who profited in selling shady prepaid calling cards and now wanted to cooperate in the hopes they would not be indicted. Since many had never seen or spoken to a Secret Service agent, they were worried. Some were even a bit "starstruck" at first and wanted to impress me with their knowledge and provided information in hopes to meet me and my colleagues so they could brag that they had rubbed shoulders with the Secret Service. They all hoped that after connecting with me, they might be privy to gossip about the president or first lady, which of course, never happened.

Prepaid card sellers provided bits and pieces of information related to the scheme, and as I listened to them, I eventually emerged as an expert in the field.

After I accumulated all that was available from the "streets," understanding every angle and various schemes associated with the prepaid calling card business, I brought those cooperating witnesses, one by one, into the Secret Service field office for an interview. It was then they realized for the first time that the jig was up.

I received my first break on the case with an attorney, Meric Bloch, who worked for AT&T. Meric was amazing. He patiently provided details and information on the telecommunications industry—specifically, the prepaid calling card business—and he helped me formulate the hypothesis associated with the fraud scheme. Since this fraud scheme had no previous history of prosecutions, the fraud was particularly difficult to piece together.

I continued reviewing the transcripts of intercepted conversations, conversing daily with Meric, and interviewing scores of witnesses, some of whom were eventually converted to cooperating witnesses. I formulated a common thread to the fraud scheme: there was a supply chain of various fraudsters who knowingly sold fraudulent cards on one end and did not pay the carriers on the other end. The carriers were also controlled to some degree by the Mafia.

The victims were the telecommunications giants and the less fortunate consumers.

As I continued the investigation, it became clear that we needed to determine an approximate dollar amount of prepaid calling cards printed and try to compare it to the international time contracted to resellers like Tel Central, which was in bed with the Mafia. This company was owned by the famous former Major League Baseball (MLB) pitcher Denny McLain.

In 1968, McLain became the last pitcher in the MLB to win 30 or more games during a season where he went 31–6, a feat that was accomplished by only 11 players in the twentieth century.

McLain had an impressive professional baseball career. However, his downfall began very early during his career. In February 1970, *Sports Illustrated* and *Penthouse* magazines both published articles about McLain's involvement in bookmaking activities. In the *Sports Illustrated* article, an alleged source explained that McLain's foot injury suffered in late 1967 had been caused by an organized crime figure stomping on it for McLain's failure to pay money owed on a bet.

When I eventually located McLain, he was serving federal time for looting money from a pension fund tied to the workers of a company called Peet Packing Company. Within 18 months after the former baseball star and his partner, Rober Smigiel, purchased the business, it went bust. In 1996, McLain was convicted of stealing $3 million from the company's pension fund in addition to money laundering, conspiracy, and mail fraud. Both McLain and Smigiel were accused of allegedly using the money to pay company debts and personal expenses. When the company went under in 1995, about 185 people lost their jobs. While he was having these issues, McLain forged ahead with criminal activities and operated Tel Central, where he committed an even larger fraud.

What would be ideal would be to identify a conspiracy to commit fraud. While it was early in the investigation, that conspiracy was not only present but captured on an intercepted conversation.

In most instances, a conspiracy charge would be corroborated through a confidential informant who, if credible, would be asked to testify in court, or potentially, wear a wire to obtain the necessary proof. But after reviewing all the intercepted conversations, hundreds of hours' worth, and then finding that one conversation where John Gotti Junior described the fraud scheme in his own words, the groundwork was set in tying the Gambino crime family to a conspiracy. The reliance on a confidential informant was not necessary.

I had to approach this case much differently than if I was presently working at the Plant, actively listening to the conversations in real time. If I had to listen to conversations at the Plant, I would have performed the following: identify both old and new targets who were participants in the scheme; build the probable cause to draft the affidavits for additional wiretaps targeting the new targets, and their locations, mobile devices, and vehicles used by the new targets; conduct active surveillance in several new locations within New York state, and crossing state lines in places like Florida and Michigan. Once those wiretap and surveillance teams were in place, I executed strategic search warrants with several goals, such as tickling the bugs for a response, seizing cash, and collecting any and all financial records available.

Instead, I had limited opportunity to do as I described. Rather, I was forced to work with the collected intercepted conversations, identify key personnel in the industry who could help me answer some of the gaps present in the intercepts, spend numerous hours vetting information provided by the cooperating witnesses, and attempt to locate, if available, any and all proof and/or data that could provide evidence to the dollar amount of fraud committed by the scheme.

Whenever a search warrant seemed feasible, I found creative ways to update the probable cause, and once that was accomplished, a warrant was issued enabling us to seize the evidence. Whenever a computer was seized, we analyzed the information on it and shared our findings with the OCTF. Based on all the investigative steps taken, I came across a main thug who was indirectly associated with the conspiracy conversation that was intercepted in 1996 between Gotti Junior and Plomitallo. This main player who took the conspiracy beyond simple conversation was Denny McLain.

Throughout the intercepted conversations, there were brief mentions of Denny McLain and Tel Central Communications, a reseller of international phone time that operated from Michigan. It was clear that Tel Central was important to the Liberty Tel prepaid calling card, which was owned by John Gotti Junior.

As in every business, efficiency was a topic of conversation, and in this case, we had intercepted the syndicate and the concern they had with McLain's equipment, in particular, the switches.

The switches were part of the telecommunications system that allowed the phone cards—purchased by consumers—to connect to the network access. This usage port allowed card–holders to make the international calls. It was basically the "highway" for phone traffic to flow.

In addition to McLain being a topic of conversation, we heard another name, "Eli." Elias "M" of Brooklyn immediately became important to the case and eventually was made a target of the investigation, since he was connected to both the earlier scheme with the Travel Card, and now with Denny McLain, he was selling the Smile & Dial card.

As stated earlier, the Travel Card case was absorbed as part of my investigation, and I had information that pointed toward Eli and the group associated with Conetco, otherwise known as Communications Network Corporation. Therefore, Eli would eventually be interviewed and later was targeted through an undercover operation on him and his illegal business activities. Both his statements and the undercover operation proved to be successful and provided an understanding of the underground world and its involvement with the prepaid telecommunication industry.

Going back to the infamous May 28, 1996, intercepted conversations between Gotti and Plomitallo, we understood that Gotti did not want to see his plans disrupted as they had been for the Travel Card. With a little digging, it was understood the company behind the travel phone card was Conetco.

In that conversation, we heard Gotti discuss organizing national brokers and distributors so that they had total control of the distribution and the cards being sold. He explained how Frank Cali, who reported to Gambino mobster, John D'Amico, would help them start up his own phone card. On March 13, 2019, Frank Cali was killed, but at the time I was investigating, he was the head of the Gambino crime family.

* * *

Conetco began selling phone cards in the summer of 1995, and by the spring of 1996, it was activating over $20 million worth of cards a month. By late 1996, Conetco declared bankruptcy, leaving WorldCom, one of the nation's largest long-distance carriers, with an unpaid balance of $94 million.

Other reputed Gambino mobsters were also tied to the firm, including Joseph "Joe the German" Watts and John "Jackie the Nose" D'Amico. Watts, who pleaded guilty in 1996 to disposing of a body in connection with the Gambino family slaying, was allegedly a mob "trailblazer" in phone scams. Within several intercepted conversations of Eli and McLain, I decided to find a vulnerability within this elaborate scheme.

I readily admit that finding the connection and understanding the scheme was not easy. No one knew what we had, absolutely no one. In fact, as mentioned earlier, the Manhattan DA's squad immediately surrendered their case to me when they heard the Secret Service was investigating phone cards.

No one in the Secret Service, FBI, nor industry was able to explain to me the actual fraud scheme. It required unprecedented investigative hours dedicated to slowly unraveling all the pieces associated with the fraud, and then repackaging those pieces and categorizing the various steps associating the folks who committed them. The ultimate goal was proving beyond a reasonable doubt that they committed the fraud. I thrived in the meticulous and mundane details of figuring out the complexity and linking all the pieces together.

At first, I focused on the actual PINs that were associated with each prepaid card and listed on the back side of each card. This led nowhere. I attempted to associate the 800 number also found on the back of the card and used that to make a link, but it turned out to be a dead end as well. What eventually surfaced from all the probing, trial and error, was that the phone card had to belong to a company, a reseller of international phone time. The company needed a distribution network, which was provided by the Mafia.

To expedite the distribution of the cards, one would provide international long-distance rates that were very cheap. The international long-distance rates sold to the consumer at the time were below market rate. Therefore, firms like Tel Central and Conetco, which contracted with MCI and WorldCom, ramped up their usage by selling the international time below market rates to prepaid calling card companies like Liberty Tel. Resellers of international time, like Denny McLain, had no intention of paying the carrier in full because the formula of selling below the purchase made no sense otherwise. Thus, selling international time below market rates made perfect sense only to folks like the ex-pitcher and to the Gambinos.

Interviews with Denny McLain's bookkeeper and mistress, and a key family member, helped unravel the fraud scheme. What I didn't know at that time was that the FBI, in early 1997 while I started my investigation, interviewed people who shared information about the phone card business and how members of the New York syndicates were involved in the prepaid calling card business. Since the FBI had other interests, they focused their attention on Walt Pavlo, a former employee of MCI. Pavlo, who has since been convicted, had created a scheme to defraud the fraudsters who had taken MCI for millions.

One such individual was Denny McLain, who through his firm, Tel Central, owed MCI approximately $30 million. It would have been ideal if all the investigators shared information to arrest the perpetrators. However, the FBI did not volunteer or provide any assistance to me. As a result, my case suffered from the lack of interagency cooperation.

Through independent sources, it became clear that Gene Lombardo, a member of the Bonanno crime family, was involved in the prepaid calling card business, and that he was receiving time for his cards from Tel Central Communications. Tel Central was Denny McLain's company, and he had an exclusive contract with MCI. Why was the FBI investigating prepaid calling cards at the same time I was? More importantly, why didn't the White Plains FBI office (the office that Echo helped by sharing Scores evidence) return the favor? Unfortunately, the FBI worked only one way and that way was always for their self-interest.

At the time, I looked for guidance and a layout of how the scheme worked, but no one had ever investigated anyone for this exact type of scheme, and thus, there were no prosecutions. The Manhattan DA had attempted to investigate Conetco Corporation, doing business as Communication Network Corporation, a New York–based company. This reseller committed approximately $90 million of phone card fraud through the Travel prepaid calling card. Conetco was where John Gotti Junior had planned to take his business, but since they had gone out of business, the OCTF wiretaps had secretly intercepted their plans to not do as Conetco did, but rather, be more versatile and fluid through Denny's firm, Tel Central.

The Tel Central fraud was committed with cards such as MVP, Smile & Dial, and Liberty Tel. Conetco, the "godfather" of prepaid calling card fraud, was owned by Vincent Rosillo and Al Khatib, and they had folks like Elias "M," Alphone "Allie Shades" Malangone, and Joe "the German" Watts all either on the payroll or working as distributors of the prepaid cards. What is important to note is these folks were not just regular businessmen; some were "made" members of the Mafia and related associates. Made Mafia are those who are formally inducted into the mob. In the end, I targeted those who spoke or were mentioned on the wiretaps.

Once Denny McLain became a main target of the investigation, I directed my efforts to investigate anyone who could be supporting his activities. I interviewed the bookkeeper, Elias, and the family member who will be unnamed. I determined the roles each and every one of these individuals played. After crafting my findings, I pitched the idea to Vince and Carroll, and in the end, they deferred to my judgment.

Toward the end of my review, I had developed extensive leads, who provided confidential sources, some dirty, some almost dirty, and others who decided, smartly, to help me lay out the scheme. These leads also pointed me in the right direction where search warrants were executed, which resulted in finding thousands of printed phone cards and storage facilities filled with worthless cards that had been shut down for nonpayment.

After my inquiries as to why the old phone cards had been kept, my informants indicated that "the directive handed down was to hold on to those printed cards because they would be reused once reactivated." In the name of Mafia efficiency and cost effectiveness to avoid reprinting more cards, evidence was preserved, waiting for me to snatch it up.

After raiding a storage facility and pulling out hundreds of boxes with thousands of prepaid cards in each, the special agent-in-charge indirectly asked me how long we would have to store all the evidence, obviously concerned with the storage costs.

Not everyone was dirty and not every distributor was connected to the scheme, but they were all part of the package to move cards at a rapid rate when directed. The Mafia controlled all the distribution. And everyone knew that if you didn't somehow participate, you and your business would pay for it, one way or another.

As I moved the case forward and began connecting the dots, I reevaluated the key intercept between Gotti Junior and Anthony Plomitallo. In that conversation, Gotti explained that what had occurred with the Travel Card and its unexpected demise would not happen with his Liberty Tel card because he would have numerous phone card companies in place to replace any phone card that was turned off. Like a dam with a leak, he would be ready to plug the hole with another card. The intercepted conversation was the foundation that explained the plan to defraud, and the beauty of such an intercept provided me the ability to connect both the fraud committed by Liberty Tel, other prepaid calling cards, and Tel Central Communications.

We charged Gotti and his associates with a conspiracy to commit fraud: 18 USC 1029; and if the case had gone to trial, all we needed to provide was evidence beyond a reasonable doubt that a conspiracy did take place. Nonetheless, my investigation in the phone card case continued to develop evidence. I collected additional evidence by interviewing new witnesses, developing key confidential informants, and conducting a successful undercover operation against a key target.

The initial wiretaps that Echo brought over to the Secret Service enabled us to identify the connection of Conetco and its questionable characters, like Joe Watts and Allie Shades, to other criminal elements associated with Tel Central, like Denny McLain, Anthony Plomitallo, Michael Zambouros, and Gotti Junior. It all came into place later through the help of informants and cooperating witnesses who enabled me to realize that some of the folks who participated with the Conetco scam had moved on and were now involved with the Tel Central folks.

On January 21, 1998, the Secret Service and OCTF planned and coordinated "Operation Ricochet." This action involved leading teams of the FBI, NYPD, and IRS to execute 30-plus simultaneous arrests of members and associates of the Gambino crime family, including John Gotti Junior.

## 10 Operation Ricochet and the Aftermath

I was dispatched to arrest John Gotti Junior with Bronx DA Detective Sergeant. Investigator Frank Thorpe. It was a cold morning in Oyster Bay, Long Island. The press camped out in front of Junior's home with their TV cameras and lights. Of course, Junior was not there, but we needed to confirm it. The FBI had requested SWAT teams for these types of arrests and wanted to make a production out of arresting him. Echo would not have any part of it. I believe he did everything he could to undermine their production. At the time, he kept his plans to himself, but recently did he share his plans with me.

Thorpe and I were tasked to go to Gotti's Oyster Bay residence and see if Junior was there. Echo made it clear from the start that he did not want this to be a circus and seeing that the FBI wanted to make it such, he called Richard Rehbock, Junior's attorney. Echo requested that Rehbock have Junior surrender at a location that made sense to everyone. Word about the conversation got back to Vince Heintz. It threw Vince into such a frenzy that he immediately went to Mitch Lambert, Echo's boss at the time, and asked for him to be fired.

Why was Echo so upset and determined to get this arrest of John Gotti Junior over with? The main reason was that Echo, a seasoned investigator with a keen sense of smelling bullshit from a mile away, had reached his limit of frustration with the FBI. In addition to my own experience of nonsense with the FBI, Echo had dealt with it throughout most of the Gambino investigation.

Echo, Vince, and OCTF senior management wanted to do the right thing by sharing information with the FBI. The result of this good will? It was exactly what the FBI has been known to do. The FBI withheld information about the case. According to Echo, his frustration with the FBI grew due to their lack of partnership, information sharing, and subtle attempts to take over the case.

One reason to send me and Thorpe to the residence was our attire. I wore a dark suit under a long, black overcoat that did not indicate any relationship to law enforcement. And Thorpe dressed the same. When we arrived on the scene, the news reporters did not give us a second glance. They never suspected we were the feds and assumed we were wise guys in the background. I walked up to the gate and spoke to the caretaker who spoke Italian and asked him if "*il padrone era a casa?*" He responded in Italian, "No, the owner is not home," and on that note, I nodded in thanks for his attention and walked back to the car.

The press ignored us because they assumed Thorpe and I were gangsters, and why would anyone want to get in the way of a gangster? Their presumption lasted until we opened our car door, which exposed our police light for all to see. Someone yelled, "Oh shit, they're cops." Within seconds, the cameras turned on us. We had just enough time to enter our vehicle and lock the doors while putting the car in reverse and peeling away from the onslaught of reporters.

As we headed back to the Armory, we waited in an unmarked police vehicle when Echo received a call from Vince. Echo explained that Richard Rehbock, Gotti Junior's attorney, was coordinating the surrender through the U.S. Attorney's Office. When the call came, Echo had offered me the honor of handcuffing Gotti Junior, a major gesture to me. However, this would not transpire.

We learned minutes later that FBI agent Jack and my boss had Gotti Junior secured and were transporting him to the Armory. The two were bringing Gotti Junior into processing, and the press photographed the three entering the building. My boss, who opportunistically wore a raid jacket for the cameras, would brag about "his" leadership in the arrest in the years that followed.

The arrest of Gotti Junior and the successful investigation into his crew was one outcome of which I am proud.

For the arrest day, the FBI volunteered fingerprint technicians, and, of course, no one saw any issue with using their technicians. Operation Ricochet involved the simultaneous arrest of 45 members/associates of the Gambino crime family. The OCTF and Secret Service had agreed that the lead arresting agency would be the Secret Service. However, I quickly realized that the FBI technicians used FBI fingerprint cards with the Region of Interest number identifying the arresting agency as the FBI. Therefore, for every "perp" that was being processed that day, no matter the charge, credit for the arrests would go to the FBI.

To counter the FBI's credit grab, I fingerprinted Gotti Junior myself on Secret Service fingerprint cards. This would ensure that when the arrest charges made it through the system, the credit went to the U.S. Secret Service and not the FBI. Top brass of the Secret Service and OCTF were involved in the entire arrest planning.

Now that Operation Ricochet was over, I realized that in a short period, a great deal was accomplished, which enabled us to expand our investigative objectives. I had joined the investigation in 1994, listening to Greg DePalma ranting and raving in his home. For a brief time, the investigation did tap his son Craig's phone, but it was believed that he was not relevant; therefore, the court order to listen in on his cell phone was not renewed. I listened to those recorded conversations again and found evidence of criminality when Craig was on the cell phone. I convinced Vince to go back up on Craig's cell phone.

A great deal was going on with Craig DePalma that was missed during the previous investigation. Although he was not as vocal as his father, Greg, he was communicating with Gotti Junior. That connection was enough to reach a level of incrimination. Part of our ability to target Gotti Junior was based on the information obtained from these cell phone conversations and surveillances, as well as from his cloned beeper, which provided the team with real-time transmittals. I fine-tuned my investigative skills prior to joining the Secret Service. These two factors helped me when I returned to the case.

Months after the round up, Vincent Heintz was on his way to work, and from the corner of his eye, he noticed Craig DePalma leaving the White Plains Courthouse and heading in a direction that did not take him directly home. Vince was a cop at heart and a former National Guard Infantry Officer. His instincts were rarely wrong.

Craig DePalma was on house detention and could only travel under specific guidelines. He was restricted from deviating his travel route between his home and the Federal Courthouse in White Plains. Vince, knowing something was amiss, initiated surveillance. At the time, I did not know he had called the FBI to assist. They declined due to not having enough advance notice. The FBI was unable to execute. So, Vince called me. He and I were very close and spoke constantly about the case. We spent hours every day discussing strategy and rehashing every aspect of the investigation. So, when he called me, I knew it was important.

I'm in my office at 7 World Trade Center, and he's in White Plains. Under normal conditions with no traffic, one would need at least 45 minutes if not an hour to get there. After Vince explained the situation, I called a loyal agent and investigator, Michael. He was assigned to the Secret Service White Plains Office.

Michael immediately grabbed his gun and jacket, then headed out to join Vince for the impromptu surveillance. Vince was on the tail; Michael was about to meet him; and I got into my blacked-out 1997 Firebird with its full police light package, a rarity in those days. I bolted out of the garage and within minutes was on the Henry Hudson Parkway heading northbound with lights flashing and sirens blaring.

I drove as fast as possible, lights and sirens all the way and with little traffic, I made it within 20–25 minutes. Michael relieved Vince, who headed to the office and, upon my direction, began to prepare a subpoena. As I approached the scene, I noticed Craig and associates were in a diner. Michael had entered, ordered some ham and eggs, and watched the suspects. I knew that the restaurant had live video surveillance recordings for security purposes. I needed this footage to bolster the field report that I would prepare later that evening.

Craig met folks from the construction industry, and we found out later it was to resolve a beef. He thought no one was watching… While they were sitting there, I walked into the restaurant unnoticed and with a quick flash of my Secret Service gold badge, I informed the manager that I needed his recorded video surveillance and that a subpoena would be provided shortly. He assured me that the surveillance video would be provided as soon as the subpoena was delivered. I thanked him and returned to my vehicle. Craig was in violation of his court-ordered detention, and for this, he would soon realize how painful this mistake would be to the Gambino crime family.

If this violation had happened 2 or 3 days prior, I would have been unable to participate because I was working a protection assignment. The life of a Secret Service agent was that our dual missions at times disrupt the continuity of our investigations. Although Michael was great, he did not have the institutional knowledge of the case necessary to make decisions based on incoming information that changed rapidly. Surveillance from the restaurant led us to the home of Craig's girlfriend, where he had approved house detention—an apartment in the Bronxville area, Westchester County.

As Craig pulled into the underground garage of the apartment complex and once I received a green light from Vince, who was now at the U.S. Attorney's Office, I hit the lights and siren. I "lit him up," as they say, and he stopped his car. After introducing myself, I explained he was in violation of his home detention.

Michael was there supporting me. Craig whined, but I told him to park the car and "Let's go upstairs." With home detention, he had no right to privacy, and since that was the case, I searched his home. Michael provided entry security, since we did not want any problems or distractions.

While searching his apartment, I feigned a need to make an urgent business call. Normally, I would have used the house phone, but instead, I pulled out my flip phone. The real reason for this maneuver was to see how Craig made and received calls with his superiors within the Gambino crime family. I soon realized that inside the apartment, cell coverage was weak to nonexistent. I made a statement to no one in particular but in a loud voice about "the fucking poor reception in this place" and being unable to make a cell call. I looked at Michael and offered a small but noticeable smile, letting him know I had a plan. I couldn't believe it. Craig responded from the couch with "Go to the kitchen and lean out the window. That's where I get the best reception."

At that point, I knew cell phones were being used between Craig and his associates. Within minutes of him making that statement, during the search, I located a cell phone in the kitchen hidden behind dishes.

The girlfriend arrived and did nothing but scream, curse, and complain about the feds always harassing her boyfriend. She entered the bathroom, then attempted to leave the apartment, but not without a search of her purse. I found the cell phone Craig was using, which we were able to prove with the call records. During my subsequent interview of the girlfriend, it all came full circle, as she was unable to explain away or tell me to whom those phone calls were made.

Once I got to the bedroom, the exciting stuff began. I found $20,000 in cash (another violation) and photos of him, the girlfriend, and another man in some of the most sadistic sexual acts I had never before or since seen. The Gambino family got another taste of the Secret Service, and I can tell you they were not accustomed to such aggressiveness.

By the end of 1998, the core team investigating the Gambino crime family comprised Vince, Vinney, Davie, Echo, and myself. Our expertise made us second to none. Whenever a voice was heard over an intercepted conversation, the name of who was speaking and whom he was associated with would be made available from memory in a matter of seconds. At that time, we were considered, among our peers, as a modern-day version of *The Untouchables*. It seemed all was going well, until the investigative team received a series of setbacks that required our attention.

## 11 The Evidence and the Plea Deal

The urgency from the prosecution team to get a plea deal had overshadowed the goal of serving justice. If convicted of a fraud, the Gambinos and Gotti Junior would have had to pay restitution. By having the phone card investigation part of the overall indictment, it forced the Gambino crime family to accept a plea, but a plea deal would exclude the fraud perpetrated against the poor folks using the phone cards and the telecommunications industry. A plea deal would avoid a trial and put away the Gambinos for overall crimes of racketeering; however, it would exempt the Mafia from paying restitution. It would be a blow to the hard work and dedication the Secret Service had committed to the investigation.

*New York Post* Article; Al Guart, March 12, 1999
**"Feds Drop Phone Rap From Gotti Indictment"**
Federal prosecutors yesterday dropped phone-card-scam charges from a massive racketeering indictment against John A. "Junior" Gotti. But prosecutors said the action would have no effect on the remaining charges accusing Gotti of running the Gambino crime family, extorting money from the topless club Scores, and robbing a drug dealer at gunpoint. His trial is set to

begin early next month. Junior, who the feds say has been running his Dapper Dad's mob interests while the elder Gotti serves a life term in prison, called yesterday's action a victory. "I was a victim. I lost a lot of money on that deal," Junior told the Post in federal court in White Plains. Gotti had been charged along with three others, including former Cy Young Award-winning pitcher Denny McLain, with selling bogus, prepaid phone cards that soaked consumers for millions.

But that aspect of the case began to fall apart when federal investigators started looking into phonecard fraud allegations against at least one large telecommunications company—and it appeared that Junior himself may have been the victim of a rip-off. The charges were not dropped against McLain and two others.

**New York Daily News, William Rashbaum, Jan. 11, 1998 "Mob Dials Up Phone Cards"**
Organized crime is muscling into the tele-communications industry, plundering millions of dollars from industry giants and picking the pockets of consumers. Mob-linked firms including one controlled by John (Junior) Gotti have made big scores with pre-paid phone cards, court papers, and law enforcement sources say. The alleged scams are being investigated by two federal grand juries. The phonecard industry is

ripe for corruption, having mushroomed to an estimated $2 billion last year from $40 million in 1993, authorities say. "It's better than drugs, because they're making so much money and the penalties are zip," a veteran organized crime investigator said. Phone cards enable callers to buy local or long-distance time in denominations ranging from $5 to $100.

They are distributed by firms that have purchased access to phone systems like WorldCom and MCI. The cards are widely available in convenience stores, newsstands, and other outlets. They are particularly popular with students and in immigrant communities because they often offer cheap rates for calls to specific countries. In a typical scam, a phonecard firm contracts with a long-distance provider, sells thousands of cards to consumers, then doesn't pay the phone system which in turn, deactivates the customers' cards. One company Communications Network Corp. (Conetco) began selling phone cards in the summer of 1995, and by spring of 1996, it was activating $20 million worth of cards a month.

When it went bankrupt late in 1996, it left WorldCom, the nation's No. 4 long-distance carrier, holding the bag for $94 million. A Brooklyn federal grand jury is investigating the alleged fraud. Sources say the firm was a front for the Gambino crime family now headed by Gotti. Other reputed Gambino mobsters tied to the firm include Joseph (Joe the German) Watts and John (Jackie the Nose) D'Amico, sources say. Watts, who pleaded guilty in 1996 to disposing of a body in connection with a Gambino family slaying, allegedly is a mob trailblazer in phone scams. Watts' lawyer, James La Rossa, acknowledged that his client worked for Conetco as a sales agent. But LaRossa said any fraud occurred after his client went to jail in 1996. "From every bit of information I have, his involvement was completely legitimate, and the company was running appropriately," LaRossa said. "And if there were thefts, they were after he left." Watts was paid $668,000 in commissions including $395,000 after he was imprisoned, court records show. Bankruptcy papers say $45 million in Conetco funds are missing. When the firm shut down more than a thousand small merchants and untold numbers of consumers were left with cards that didn't work. "We lost $200; for us that's a lot of money," said Mohamed Saker, a Brooklyn man who owns a newsstand at the Rockaway Parkway subway stop on the L line, and retailed Conetco's cards. "The guy that sold it to us disappeared."

An unrelated federal grand jury in White Plains is hearing evidence about Gotti's phonecard company as part of a broader probe into the alleged mobster and the construction industry. Gotti's lawyer, Richard Rehbock, said his client has committed no crimes. He said authorities "have interfered incredibly with his legitimate pursuits," and claimed Gotti's firm lost money because investigators seized 13,000 phone cards. "They would like very much to throw a marquee name into an indictment," Rehbock said. Gotti's card company, formed in the spring of 1996 and no longer operating, was called Nic O Dan Communications and was run by his one-time driver, Anthony Plomitallo.

A source said Gotti's company took MCI and two other long-distance carriers for more than $50 million in a scam in which they ran up bills and sold discounted cards before they were shut down. The state Organized Crime Task Force and the Secret Service raided the firm in February and again in October, seizing business records, computers, and thousands of Liberty Tel cards, which have the Statue of Liberty emblazoned on their faces. Secret Service agents also executed a search warrant in November at a Florida company that manufactured the cards for Gotti's firm. That company, Ameriplast, is not a target of the probe. Court papers said investigators were seeking any documents or business records linked to Liberty Tel, Gotti, Plomitallo, or a number of other people and companies. An official at Ameriplast said 26 agents spent nine or 10 hours at his company and went through its computerized record system.

Those two articles in New York City's most favored newspapers tell a tale of two cities. They represent the highs and lows of this investigation and represent a whole lot more than just the words used to convey what happened. I realized to my great disappointment that all the hard work and dedication placed into identifying the scheme and collecting the necessary evidence was now going to be dropped due to the plea negotiations.

Whenever I read articles written about how charges on a case are dropped, it is painful. No matter how many times I have read the press coverage over the years since the investigation, I remain angry over the information presented to the public. The very article that was written approximately a year earlier, lays out the scheme and mentions several members of the syndicate, including Gotti Junior, as key players. This was not a one-time fraud. It was an attack by the Mafia on an industry. Nevertheless, the fraud I identified was specific and in the end was quite simple to prove.

Why then were the charges against the head of the Gambino crime family dropped? Most likely, the charges were dropped because John Gotti Junior, when negotiating his plea deal, wanted nothing to do with restitution. If convicted, the amount he would need to pay in restitution would be staggering. In the syndicate, the loss of money weighs supreme over all other options. Mobsters look at doing time in prison as part of doing business; it is a cost they are willing to pay.

Typically in law enforcement, if a criminal is caught in only one great scheme, the offender negotiates a prison sentence of a decade or less in prison, but the stolen money awaits for the criminal upon his release. We indicted Gotti Junior and associates with a conspiracy charge. The suspects were clearly intercepted over the government bugs discussing a bust-out scheme, and admitting to past performance as well as future plans to do the same.

A conspiracy charge, however, brings challenges to a defense team. A conspiracy is a broad crime that can sweep up many kinds of conduct. Typically these types of charges are a big challenge to defend in court. A federal criminal defense attorney, who has a client charged with conspiracy, has to be very diligent in investigating the government's evidence and what role the government thinks each person had in the conspiracy. This can be a daunting task.

The general federal conspiracy statute 18 U.S.C. 371 criminalizes conspiracies to defraud the United States as well as conspiracies to violate any other provision of federal law. A conspiracy to commit a federal crime happens whenever there is an agreement to commit a specific federal crime between two or more people. And at least one of those people engages in an overt act to further the conspiracy.

The government does not have to prove that there was a written agreement between the coconspirators; instead, the prosecutor can prove a conspiracy just by proving that the people it says were involved were working together to commit some crime.

The courts have held that an individual can be in a conspiracy with another person, even if the two people never meet or interact, as long as they knew the other person was doing something to further the conspiracy. Denny McLain repeatedly stated during his meetings with me that he never met Gotti, and of course, I didn't comment, since I knew what the conspiracy statute stated on use of such a defense. Of course, not ever meeting your coconspirators is most common in a larger, sprawling conspiracy where a central person, or group, and/or enterprise such as the "syndicate," would coordinate the work of others.

* * *

A conspiracy charge has the potential to be abused by the government. Taken to absurd consequences in theory, a conspiracy offense could be committed and prosecuted in federal court merely by having two people agree that they would rob a bank together, then buy a ski mask to wear in the bank robbery. But the syndicate did a lot more than just buy a ski mask.

One vicious consequence of a conspiracy charge is that a minor participant in a conspiracy can be swept up in the same case as someone who is much more culpable for criminal conduct. This is a particularly bad problem in drug conspiracy cases. For example, a person who had a very minor role in a drug conspiracy that involved a significant quantity of drugs can be subject to a mandatory minimum for all the drugs in the conspiracy.

In our case, we have John Gotti Junior discussing the scheme with Anthony Plomitallo on a bug that was planted in a vehicle driven by Plomitallo. We recorded numerous discussions about the distribution capabilities and the recruitment of those who were considered not only good distributors but also played well with others in the "criminal sandbox." The key players in the prepaid phone card scam were folks like Denny McLain, Joe "the German" Watts, and Salvatore Scala, to name just a few.

These were career criminals who had been doing bad things for a long time. The beauty of the wiretaps and bugs planted by OCTF was that John Gotti Junior felt comfortable and compelled to discuss the scheme to his driver at a time that was critical to moving the scheme forward. Travel Cards had just defrauded WorldCom of over $90 million, and they had to file for bankruptcy since they were shut off. Since the scheme went well, they decided to continue it and included other players in the mix. One key player was Denny McLain and his company, Tel Central.

As Gotti Junior explained, whenever a card had issues of potentially being shut down due to non-payment, the Mafia would issue a new card. Once the service was cut off, the scheme had no life, and it had no choice but to terminate. This $90 million one-time fraud scheme had the Gambino crime family all excited.

In fact, even the late John Gotti Senior commented in prison about the phone card business. When one of Senior's sons, Peter, told him, "Dad, I'm in the phone card business," Gotti Senior laughed and said, "What a scam."

We had additional intercepts that mentioned the association of the syndicate with Denny McLain and how he was preparing to ramp up service for them. In a written confession and as a cooperating witness, we had Denny's unnamed family member outline the scheme.

The investigative work was done mostly by me and a few other novice agents. No one in the New York Field Office had any experience involving a long-term fraud investigation that targeted the head of an organized crime syndicate. Special Agent "Chris" was my only partner, and like me, had no reason to go home and watch movies. We loved the hunt investigations offered, and prior to Chris joining, I was working this unknown fraud alone. What was especially frustrating was the lack of guidance provided to me by the Secret Service. In their defense, they were just too busy with the protection services.

Adopting the dual mission practice disrupted the continuity of investigations, especially when I had come from such a long-term investigative culture. For instance, in the Secret Service there was a good understanding of how a search warrant should be conducted, but how to get there within the fraud arena, a very limited amount of experience existed among the senior agents. The Service in New York was good with conducting counterfeit cases. This was because the mentality used was strictly buy-and-bust operations. They would dedicate themselves for 2-3 weeks of tireless investigative efforts toward an operation, and hopefully, a protection assignment would not derail the momentum. If one did, it would more likely than not put the case on the back burner. Unless the suspect reappeared, it was closed out.

Proactive investigative work was a foreign concept during this time unless it involved a protective intelligence case. The Service expended great effort, time, and resources to conduct thorough investigations toward those who made threats against the president or any person under the Service's protection. The stakes were too high for it to be otherwise.

During my time in the Secret Service, starting a case from the ground up (selecting a known fraudster then building a criminal case that included criminal charges and asset forfeiture seizure) was rarely encouraged since the agency's protective missions took precedence. Although the agency maintained a dual mission, protective responsibilities consumed most of the available resources.

The idea of starting a case from the ground up on a known target because of the level of fraud perpetrated was easily dismissed. From my perspective, these agents were doing casework simply to stay busy until they were assigned their next protection assignment and nothing more. This was how the agency at the time was structured, and the New York Field Office was no different. The only difference was the size and location of the office. If the office was located in a major city or near the home of a former president, then the mission would have a heavy day-to-day commitment to the protection mission, but this was not the case with our investigative mission. I couldn't get one person to be fully committed to asset forfeiture and/or understand it. Yet the NYFO had an asset forfeiture squad. I often felt alone going up against a formidable opponent with little or no support.

Although asset forfeiture support within the US Secret Service was limited, I carved my own path, built credibility, and worked independently. During this time, I collaborated with a remarkable, young woman: Marie Boss, who I met at the New York State Organized Crime Task Force. She relentlessly pursued assets of the Gambino crime family and always welcomed the intelligence I uncovered through my own investigations. Marie worked quietly in the shadows, never seeking recognition, but her expertise was unmatched. When it came to following the money, she was the authority, methodical, sharp, and fearless. Watching her operate was like observing a master at work, and I was grateful for her performing that essential role.

## 12 Dual Mission: Investigations/Protection

As time passed, I slowly adapted to some of the clothing and equipment that was a staple trademark of the agency. We, Secret Service agents, all bought a particular luggage system. The features of this luggage were exceptional, and the luggage itself was extremely durable. Of course, it was all black and specifically designed for government agents who were on the road more often than not. Long-term sturdiness was the key essential behind the design. Yet, to carry it you either slung it over your shoulder or carried it by hand. They did not have wheels, and unlike flight attendant luggage that could attach additional luggage to one main piece that had wheels, we had no consolidation options.

The people who designed this luggage must have been bodybuilders who were strong enough to lift it. For agents on the road 2 to 3 weeks at a time, it was horrible. Instead, this ballistic nylon bag with pockets everywhere was designed for all sorts of weapons, ammo, pistols, rifle magazines, flashlights, and handcuffs. However, for the frequent traveler who needed to carry it from point A to point B through a crowded airport, while wearing a suit, it was impractical at best, and a hinderance at its worst. Yet for some reason, we all purchased and carried the same luggage. Go figure.

Weeks prior to any presidential trip, the Secret Service begins preparation for all aspects of security surrounding the visit. Therefore, the time that needs to be allocated for the preparation of a visit is the first challenge for agents working a case load. Although agents' protection detail was temporary, protection of dignitaries always maintained a higher priority than investigations. Therefore, no matter how critical an investigation was, we agents could be called for protection duty at any time, taking us away from the continuity of the investigation.

The agents from the Presidential Protective Division, those who surrounded the inner circle of the president, worked in partnership with the agents from various field offices to provide necessary protection whenever they were on the road. The process began with the security advance, whereby liaison was conducted with all stakeholders, including the host committee, business owners, local law enforcement, and public safety officials to ensure a cohesive and coordinated effort once the president stepped foot off Air Force One.

In August 1996, fellow agents and I were selected to serve as train security. It was not a glamorous position, or a coveted one, for that matter. I never came within 30 yards of President Clinton. Nevertheless, it was a necessary function, albeit a tedious one. It was an election year, and the president was on the way to winning his second term. As a new agent, I served in the wings, in staircases, back alleys, and along his whistle-stop tour, providing physical middle perimeter security.

Agents awoke before sunrise every day, boarded a bus that transported us to a train where we took our predetermined positions. Usually, two agents were assigned per train car. Then we waited for hours until the president boarded the train and the campaign whistle-stop began. The ride was uncomfortable, since we were not allowed to sit.

When the train stopped, crowds in the thousands gathered along the tracks to catch a glimpse of President Clinton. Crowd members waved, screamed, or occasionally carried signs expressing either love or disdain for him. Agents stood along each side of an open train car and did our best to scan the environment for threats.

We were not allowed to leave those damn train cars… So we did what we were tasked to do; namely, scan the crowds for unusual activity or abnormal behavior. If we noticed any anomaly, we called it out over the radio.

Despite the importance of protection detail, one couldn't resist the feeling of boredom sitting in those hot train cars. Yet, this feeling was replaced with a spike in adrenaline when we stopped in every small town and watched the vibrant people gather to witness a glimpse of history.

The public euphoria was at times contagious as bands played loud, upbeat music, the people happy to be a part of something greater than themselves and bigger than the small towns from where they came. What they witnessed, though, was the finished product of weeks of intense negotiations, long hours of security advance work, weeks away from home, and, of course, the mundane routine and boredom. Boredom and routine were quite often the hallmark and vulnerability of an agent's work on protection; yet, we all found it within ourselves to fight the dangers of complacency to again be vigilant once the train stopped and the doors opened.

I experienced my first real investigative withdrawal and sense of competition for my time while on protective security detail. One day I am working the streets; then abruptly on another day, I am standing on a train car wearing a suit and an earpiece that is connected to a handheld radio. How can this be? I remember asking myself these very questions. If you're working a case, deeply involved in an investigation, how do you just walk away and do something totally different and basically have no contact with suspects, witnesses, or government attorneys, and be considered a real investigator?

* * *

I saw the value and higher purpose in the protection mission, but felt that the continuous interchange between protective and investigative assignments prevented one from fully immersing themselves in the intricacies of a complex investigation. Regardless of the protection demands, I continued to make and close cases, usually during my "off-duty" hours.

After the Gotti investigation, my protection orders came to help safeguard the fifth president of the People's Republic of China, Jiang Zemin's visit to New York City to meet with the POTUS. Manpower was needed for protection work; since my investigation of the Gotti crime syndicate was over, I no longer could use it as a reason to delay or avoid protective services.

In one assignment, I spent 4 days on 12-hour shifts standing in the fire stairwell of the Waldorf-Astoria hotel. During those very long hours in a hot stairwell, with nothing to do but think, I quickly realized that my opportunity working sophisticated cases had come to an end.

During these painfully mundane and long days, I was accompanied by various police officers of the New York city Police Department's (NYPD) Emergency Services Unit, an elite tactical team. I never had the same officer twice given that the NYPD had 38,000 officers at the ready. Each time I spoke to a newly assigned officer to my post, I was thrilled that we had an hour or so of discussions before that new experience came to an end. The extremely tedious part came after the initial hour, when there was nothing more to ask each other. At that point, both the officer and I would retreat to opposite corners where there was partial light so that if we rested a bit by closing our eyes, while standing, no one would catch us in the act. The hours spent in that stairwell were painful, especially for someone like me whose mind always raced. This was a slow death sentence, and I was unwilling to accept it.

At times, I would count various things to keep busy, such as cracks on the stairs—anything to pass the time.

The hours seemed to never pass when on such assignments, and it had been some time since I had actually stood for so long. I would try to think of so many things just to keep myself occupied.

Then there were problems at home that would grind at you. I never had that issue but did see agents go on post, and as they would be heading to their assignment, you could overhear them discuss the problem at home on a phone, and it would end with, "Hey, I got to go. Call you tomorrow." No one really had any privacy when they were on post.

* * *

After the Gotti Junior case, I was promoted by ATSAIC Weaver—assistant to the special agent in charge—to be one of his team leaders in the squad. I was very proud of the acknowledgment and excited to help new agents who wanted to work criminal cases. We had a mix of agents from the private sector, state, and local law enforcement agencies with a broad range of experiences. One thing about the New York Field Office…No one stayed for long since the protection machine always required fresh blood, and folks were constantly assigned to a respective detail. The typical career track had you going from the field office to a protection detail, to headquarters, then back to a field office, or return to protection.

Since the Gotti case was over, my hands-off status that allowed me to work investigative cases and not be available for temporary protection assignments, was also over. Therefore, every time a case came across my desk, I had just enough time to assign it or deal with it ineffectually for a day or two. Weaver knew that I was getting frustrated and reminded me that my time was coming to an end in the office and unless I opted out, which meant stay in New York, and embarked on the typical Secret Service career path, I would be given assignments to get me ready and exposed to either the Presidential Protective Division or the Vice Presidential Protective Division.

Since I was not interested in protection, I looked for ways to distance myself from the work. At the time, a program existed that was directed to larger field offices that allowed an agent to opt out and stay in New York for one's entire career. Although I was no longer in the running for a promotion, this program exempted me from doing full-time protection. However, it also sent a negative message about me to Washington, and my temporary protection assignments did not end. I was still part of a rotation like all the other 200-plus agents in New York. As a result, this attractive option did not completely satisfy my highest interests, which were to solve sophisticated, long-term financial crime cases that involved the Mafia.

I plugged along. Days turned into weeks, which turned into months. I worked various financial crime cases and random protective assignments. 1998 ended with a mix of foreign dignitary protection assignments, working post-standing assignments for President Clinton and Vice President Gore, and on a personal note, getting a divorce.

In early 1999, I received a call from one of the private sector contacts within the utility industry. He informed me that his utility company was having an issue in Harlem with some unusual activity at a particular apartment.

Someone was using the utility service illegally. After speaking with Weaver and securing permission, I assigned the case to my partner Chris and another fairly new agent who was talented in cybersecurity, Peter Cavicchia. Chris had been my partner at Electric Crimes Task Force (ECTF). We both had apartments in Riverdale, New York. He had served in the military and was active during the Persian Gulf War. Chris was the nephew to the director of the Secret Service, Lew Merletti, a fact he never discussed or tried to exploit.

The case involved a West African ring that used stolen credit cards to purchase long-distance phone time as well as merchandise. As the team leader, I provided guidance and direction, but my satisfaction came from seeing this new wave of younger agents think through the investigative process and make sound decisions. We presented the case to Assistant U.S. Attorney Eric Bruce and Michael Kim, two outstanding attorneys who work together at a very successful law firm in Manhattan.

In my investigative world as a case agent, I would track the finances and work up the food chain to see who was running the operation. By going down this road and influencing the agents to do the same, I knew that it would be a terrible mistake. The Service would make a mess of the case by disrupting the investigative process with protective assignments.

I kept my opinions to myself and coached the agents to keep cases small, focus on immediate targets, and close cases. This went completely against my investigative grain. However, I had no choice but to do so since the agency was not geared for a marathon investigation—one where the investigative strategy and the identification of assets from the criminal proceeds were the focus. I knew that any attempt to conduct a long-term investigation would result in failure.

* * *

We were trying to obtain evidence to execute a search warrant at this apartment in Harlem where most of the residents within a two-block radius were from West Africa. The target, at the time, was unknown but in the end through standard checks, we identified the main suspect as Seck Seynabou. She was a woman from Africa and the listed tenant of the apartment. Seck was later identified as one of the fraudsters. On our initial surveillance of the location, we noticed from the exterior part of the building an unusual phone line connected to others and running through the window to her apartment.

We had with us a phone company representative, who was also a task force member. He helped identify that someone was tapping into the phone lines of other legitimate customers. With our partnerships in the private sector, it was clear this line was not authorized. Now we needed to gain entry to get a glimpse of the situation inside and obtain enough probable cause to secure a search warrant.

Chris and I posed as Consolidated Edison (ConEd, an energy company) workers; our squad had the equipment and the IDs in storage, so why not? We had a simple plan, usually the best way…We go to each apartment and count the rooms and square footage so we can supply free air conditioners… It was the middle of a blistering-hot summer and free window units for those that qualify sounded like a good plan.

As we made our way to the building, wouldn't you know it, an actual ConEd truck was parked 100 feet from the building entrance. We were caught by surprise. Before we could turn around and abort the operation, one of the supervisors spotted us. I approached him and shoved him back in the truck while flashing my badge. He then understood, this was not something to screw up. We got past that obstacle, then we headed to the building. The truck outside made the whole thing appear authentic, except for our outdated uniforms and hard hats, which were what the ConEd worker spotted.

We offered the rebate starting with the floors below the target and finished at the top floor. We did not want Seck to think she was singled out. We needed to look as real as possible. We went as far as purchasing a few

AC units in the event we needed to return to the apartment to obtain more evidence.

Once we came to the suspect's apartment, Seck opened the door. I persuaded her enough to get in. As we moved inside the apartment discussing the rebate and using measuring tape around windows, we spotted a notebook pad in plain view. Handwritten on the page were at least a dozen credit card numbers with various names and Social Security numbers. We could see numerous phone cards on the table. Connected to the mysterious line coming through the window was both a phone and fax machine. This was enough evidence for a search warrant. We thanked Seck, who was demanding her AC unit, and we promised after checking our calendar that sometime on Monday or Tuesday of next week we would have her unit delivered.

Within 48 hours, the search warrant was granted, and the operations plan completed and approved. Some agents had just completed their protection assignments and now were changing out of their suits and strapping on their unique dark blue, bulletproof vests with the gold Secret Service star on the front.

The local police precinct was notified. Since this was a task force, we had every local and federal presence within the squad. I had my entry team, my arrest and evidence team, and my outside perimeter team. We were set, and when we hit, we hit hard and fast so that no one inside the apartment had a chance to think…Hey, these were Secret Service men and women in the best shape with the best equipment. No evidence went without proper review. We arrested a total of six individuals in the apartment, including Seck, and seized thousands of compromised individual credit card accounts and hundreds of thousands of dollars of merchandise.

This was a well-organized ring of thieves and fraudsters collecting information on valid credit card holders. Some of them were customers that frequented the African stores for merchandise. Other victims were tourists who took city bus tours. But within minutes of entering, sitting on, or exiting the bus, their wallets were stolen and their credit cards compromised by this sophisticated group.

I was ready to testify for the Seck case in front of a blind judge, the Honorable Richard Conway Casey, who had his trusty Labrador that growled at the defendant whenever she spoke in French. The hearing was to determine whether the defendant would be released and allowed to surrender her passport to the court.

The defendant's attorney, Roland Thau, began by apologizing to the judge and asking for the opportunity to explain his position. He was preparing to request the courts not remand Seck but rather release her and allow her time to return and surrender her passport, which, by the defendant's statement, was nowhere to be found. To make matters worse, Roland unsuccessfully attempted to taint our reputation with an unfortunate incident that happened weeks earlier when two Secret Service agents from the New York Field Office were caught lying about a witness. The incident made the news, and it was embarrassing. Roland wanted to know if I was one of those agents.

The Honorable Judge Casey had a reputation for being pro–law enforcement and did not like the public defender's tactics. So when Roland opened his argument by asking for permission to speak, the judge immediately interrupted him and stated, "It better be good, Mr. Thau." So the moment Roland responded by saying "Am I to conclude from that short remark that the court has already..." Casey didn't allow him to finish his sentence, firing back, "You can conclude anything you want, but you're suggesting that I drop it as a condition." The exchange that followed was intense, to say the least, and I must say, I was laughing on the inside, but no one knew it.

* * *

My chapter in New York was now over. With the Gotti case behind me, and feeling a bit frustrated with the Secret Service, I called Al Concordia, a resident agent in charge in Milan, Italy. Months earlier, I was looking for hotels to stay in the area and was introduced to him by his office assistant Marisa, a wonderful woman who has since passed. She was the life of the office. Al and I immediately connected, and I asked him if the invitation to be assigned in Milan was still open. He assured me it was and after letting Weaver know of my intentions, he spoke to the special agent in charge (SAIC) in New York, Chip Smith, and the rest was history. Although Milan was not my final destination, Rome had a SAIC, and he trumped the resident agent in charge. I eventually received orders to report to Rome.

After being in Rome for about 6 months, I returned to New York City for the criminal trial of Seck. I was thrilled to be home again, since I missed my friends and girlfriends. We prepped for the case and once the trial began, we exuded a serious tone. Court started in much the same manner as our last engagement with Seck and

Roland. The court-appointed attorney, who was a disheveled older man resembling Bernie Sanders, was bent on getting that aha! moment. It was my turn on the stand. Roland peppered me with questions, hopelessly looking for some clue or break that would turn the trial in favor of his client.

Honestly, it was useless. The case was airtight, and everything we did was absolutely aboveboard. So when Roland asked his questions, I was extremely well prepared, confident, and although never cocky, I enjoyed the sparring that took place in the courtroom. Each time he asked a question, stumbling over his words at times, I turned toward the jury and provided answers while looking into the eyes of each and every juror. I fully answered his questions, providing detailed descriptions of the evidence or circumstances that led to a particular conclusion. Roland was obviously frustrated and had no choice but to concede to the loss.

The assistant United States attorney called me to thank me for my efforts. This call was followed by an official letter of appreciation sent to the New York Office and Rome Field Office. They were so pleased with the outcome; Seck was convicted on all counts.

My superiors were thoroughly convinced that the jury was not only impressed with the investigative facts, but also with my representation of the case. I didn't realize it then, but reflecting back, they were all so attentive whenever I spoke. Assistant United States Attorney Michael Kim explained that the jury during deliberations had asked to see me one more time and he had to inform them that I was on my way to Rome. Worried, he had asked if there were any concerns; however, they were basically starstruck and said, "No, we just wanted to see him one last time."

I was now officially done with my investigative work in New York. It was time to head back to Rome.

## 13 Italy and Romania

If you have not visited Rome, Italy, you need to book a trip to that wonderful city and spend a week living and eating like a real Romano! During my transfer there, I indulged in the culture. I had the advantage of my Italian upbringing in New York. Within months, I had shed all my bulky American suits and shoes and wore a scarf around my neck as if I were a native, wrapping it in a European loop. My friends made fun of me upon my return to the States for this particular newfound style. I purchased a motorcycle, one of the most luxurious racing bikes built for touring; an all-gray 2000 BMW 1200RS. At the time, I was about the only one in Rome who had one, and everyone stared at it when I rode to work wearing a matching-colored helmet.

The social gatherings in Rome were amazing, and during the summer months, U.S. embassy diplomats had access to the ambassador's pool at Villa Taverna. The ambassador's residence was within walking distance from my apartment in Parioli, a very affluent neighborhood that housed many foreign ambassadors. I was provided an apartment suited for a family of four, and being a single man, this was more than enough room. The American Embassy in Rome was located on

Via Veneto, and our annex was just a few blocks away, so although the place was secure, it was a bit less pronounced to the tourists who flocked to Via Veneto year-round.

I was assigned a government car outfitted with diplomat plates used for official duty, but on my personal time, I drove my other jewel, a red 1984 five-speed Porsche 911 Carrera. On the weekends, I switched from motorcycle to the car, depending on the weather conditions. The car was also an absolute looker, with a badass whale tail to further impress. It was completely refurbished with attention to the slightest detail. The car had a Targa top that was always off whenever I drove through the beautiful region of Italy known as La Toscana.

With custom stainless-steel Haywood & Scott Crossover exhausts letting everyone know that we were coming, it was a blast to drive. I particularly enjoyed making the doorman to my apartment building smile as I drove out of the garage and up the driveway. He kept smiling while holding his broom until I completely disappeared from view. As I made my way down the road, cars parked along the narrow road sounded their alarms, all set off from the vibration and loud rumbling coming from my pipes.

The Italian cuisine provided another intoxicating experience. Yes, I was from Italian heritage, and we cooked authentically, but there was something different coming out of the kitchens and restaurants in Rome. I enjoyed every meal and every minute. I quickly became good friends with my Italian counterparts who were also in law enforcement. Stefano, Salvatore, and Marco were all unique; they possessed great knowledge of the food and culture and wanted me to experience it too. These guys were proud to be Italian, knew exactly where to eat, and knew how not to spend a boatload of money doing so. Going to dinner with these fine men was always a spectacular time.

We always started our evening with an *aperitivo* used to entice one's appetite. Gaining an appetite was never an issue for me. The next item would be a little *assaggino*, which loosely translated means a small taste of something delicious! We usually had some perfectly cured prosciutto, which is Italian air-dried ham served thinly sliced. Typically, it was served on a wooden board that housed other mouthwatering items like homemade bread drizzled with extra virgin olive oil, local cheeses, and an assortment of other delights.

In Italy, dinner was a performance. Locals did not look for a quick bite but rather quality, and they understood what quality meant in food. The protocol in restaurant service was not to rush the guest to turn the table, but rather to give the guest an experience. Italians are also very picky about what they eat and, above all, want to enjoy their company at the table. The typical dinner was a minimum of 2-plus hours. Besides these leisurely dinners, I enjoyed watching people.

Whenever I had a weekend to myself, I spent it sitting at an outdoor café at Piazza Navone and pretended to read a newspaper, all the while checking out the locals, tourists, and those in between. It was wonderful to sit there having a cappuccino with little pastries resembling croissants called *corneti*, or during the latter part of the day grabbing a panini filled with mortadella from the local street vendor. The experience was only surpassed by the euphoria felt by supporting a foreign government law enforcement team in identifying criminals who were exploiting U.S. citizens.

It's Monday morning in Rome, Italy; I started that particular morning by quietly taking my shorts and a T-shirt. In my bed, still sleeping, was my blonde, German-born, Lufthansa flight attendant who I had met on a trip to the Middle East. Typically, I would arrange for the woman who would spend a weekend with me in Rome to leave on a Sunday night so that I could prepare for the week's mission. This time, however, I had slipped, and although I was being a bit selfish, I decided to keep my "lady friend" in Rome for an extra night. In the morning, I quickly hid my weapon and credentials and made myself a caffé macchiato prior to my 30-minute jog, followed up with a half-dozen sprints up a flight of stairs, and 100 push-ups and sit-ups. I always enjoyed the drills that caused a pouring of sweat.

After a last-minute romp in the bedroom, my friend departed by cab, and I headed off to work in my government-issued car, a late-model BMW. But not without first inspecting it with my "field-improvised" security measures. Knowing the car had been parked for the weekend, I applied countermeasures to determine if it had been compromised in any way. This was a country where car bombs were the preferred choice of eliminating enemies. After a quick review convincing me that all was good, I headed toward Fiumicino Airport to board the Alitalia flight bound for Bucharest, Romania.

Romania was a country with abject poverty. As the Alitalia flight approached the runway, I saw abandoned commercial and military airplanes that resembled roadside carcasses. They had engine parts stolen; some had parts of the fuselage missing. I could not believe they allowed this to be the first visual image experienced by the foreign visitor. However, this was Romania, and they were under communist rule. I gathered they had bigger issues to contend with, as I was soon going to find out.

Upon exiting the airport, I began my countersurveillance measures, to make it difficult to be followed. As soon as I left the airport, children of all ages surrounded me, begging for money. They were all in one way or another deformed yet all so cute. My heart broke every time I encountered them. Today, I sometimes see those faces whenever I look into the eyes of my own kids. It pained me to see these suffering children, and in the not-too-far distance, I could see their handlers. As other foreigners handed out money, the mothers approached with the goal of pickpocketing them.

The buildings were dilapidated and the means in which folks were cared for was equal to that of animals. Hospitals, dental facilities, and overall public facilities were poorly equipped, and sanitary conditions were at best, marginal.

During my travels to Bucharest, I stayed at the Hilton Hotel, and whenever I got there, I initiated a series of drills to confuse the Romanian intelligence. After receiving my set of keys, I would return to the front desk claiming the room was dirty and forced them to switch me out of the current room. Then I always left the TV on, and of course, used the Do Not Disturb sign. To ensure no one was in my room, or heading there, I used the stairs, then hopped on the elevator to quickly return to the room. In many instances, after switching rooms I found a "technician" in the room. I had obviously surprised him and his team, and although he was "working" on my TV, it was clear he was there for nefarious reasons.

I was fortunate to have a team of two Romanian law enforcement counterparts. I worked exclusively with Tibus and Cristian throughout my time there. These two men were serious investigators who protected me from corrupt Romanian officers. It was because of them that I was successful in fulfilling Special Agent in Charge Ralph Ganzalez's demand, "I want us to have a presence in Romania." And because of my two counterparts, I never felt overly concerned about my personal safety. Tibus and Cristian were based out of the Romanian police headquarters and specialized in computer crimes.

I met Tibus in his office, which took me by surprise. Here I was a U.S. Special Agent with all the latest technology and equipment, and as we can all attest to, we were always complaining about our resources, or the lack thereof. In contrast, Tibus was relegated to building his computer from various scrap parts. If you weren't informed ahead of time that it was an official government computer, you would think it was a pile of junk ready to be thrown out. With headquarters' approval, we immediately shipped Tibus some updated computer equipment.

Tibus was sincere, honest, and wanted to do good. How fortunate for me to meet such an investigator. I was then introduced to his friend, Cristian, who was from another section of the police department. Like many people in that region, he was afraid that one day their relationship with the U.S. would be disrupted by either corruption or communist hardliners. You could see the concern in their eyes, but with all that said, these men were courageous and ready to fight.

Soon after forging our friendship, we had our opportunity to work together. An agent from Secret Service headquarters called and talked about a cyber case that was originating out of Romania. The referral call went to me since I was tasked to get Romania staffed with a full-time Secret Service presence. The headquarters' agent explained that the home page to the Thrift Savings Plan was recently hacked and compromised, and the attack originated in Romania. I requested that all the details be sent to me, and within hours of the call, I made contact with the Romanian company that hosted the IP address used to violate the site.

After initiating other investigative steps as well as contacting our folks at the International Criminal Police Organization (INTERPOL), I eventually spoke with the owner of the server in Romania. In broken English, he provided me with helpful information. I contacted Tibus and explained the issue, and he was receptive. I provided copies of the data we had collected, and in a matter of hours, Tibus was certain that the incident had taken place in Timisoara, Romania, and that he was ready to travel there to interview suspects. I then briefed my boss and the folks in Washington.

After getting briefed by Tibus, I flew to the city of Timisoara where I homed in on finding the hackers. Tibus, due to political reasons, was unable to accompany me. Although only a little over an hour, it was a shocking flight. Passengers were allowed to smoke onboard. This was bad enough—until I noticed farm animals were allowed passage, including a large goat. Operated by Tarom, the old plane had curtains on the windows, the type you would find in an old country kitchen. We boarded from the rear, and I noticed that the tires on the plane had visible white threads exposed. I was completely prepared for the worst incident possible with this flight and could not wait to get off. We were flying on an old Tarom turboprop plane with a capacity of no more than 50 passengers. The entire experience was nerve-racking.

Timisoara is one of the largest cities in Romania with a little more than 300,000 inhabitants. The city was always in the center of economic development and one of the first cities in Europe to have electric streetlights. Now, in terms of living standards, it ranks fourth in the country with foreign investment always knocking on "her" door; Timisoara has had significant foreign investment. It all didn't matter in comparison to the rest of the world; it was third world at best.

Within hours of my arrival in Timisoara, I was informed that my Bucharest police team, Tibus and Cristian, would meet me the following day. I needed them as they were my only lifelines when it came to understanding the crime and finding something that would tie the crime to a punishment. Without them, we would be lost and run the risk of looking like a bunch of fools. I was doubtful in the competency and commitment of the police department officials to adequately investigate and support me. I found people I trusted and wanted them involved. I did not want to go through the normal dog-and-pony show, having to babysit government officials, wine and dine them, and in the end, be all for naught—simply a waste of my time. I wanted to get to work.

Everywhere you go in Romania, including Timisoara, you see folks begging with some horrible physical deformities. The people are known as Romani ("Roma" gypsies). I was later told not to pay any mind to those begging because it was not only depressing, but it needed to be ignored since it was really all just a big scam. The truth was their own family members deformed many of their children at birth. These people were looking for ways to make money. To gain sympathy, they did these terrible things to their own children when they were all very young. A complete tragedy, one that to this day, I still see deformed children haunting me in my dreams.

I felt for the first time powerless. How could this be? Here I am in Romania, this special agent of the Secret Service, everyone excited to see me, and the first wave of injustice hits me…and all I can do is stare hopelessly back. It was difficult.

In one instance, a child stood barefoot in the middle of the winter begging with his hands out hoping to collect some money. I grabbed him with one quick swift swoop with one arm as his father from a distance watched. I rushed him into a shoe store and as I purchased a pair of shoes for him, I slipped him one Romanian 100.000 leu (about $20), when I pretended to check how the shoes fit. The boy, now being out from the cold, with his rosy red cheeks, had a smile from ear to ear. He was happy but not for the shoes I bought him but for the money he understood was all his.

When I arrived at my hotel in Timisoara, I met the colonel and several of his men in the lobby. We ordered food and of course drinks. Despite having a translator, we accomplished very little, since he had a hard time understanding how anyone could steal anything unless they were physically present. Cybercrime was an alien concept.

Computers for these guys represented nothing more than a paperweight. I needed to bide my time until my counterparts from Bucharest arrived. What was also developing was a strong response from Secret Service headquarters. Within hours, several agents from headquarters were on a plane to join me. The headquarters support was merely more of a political presence. By the time they arrived, my Romanian counterparts had already identified the suspects, and we all drove to their homes.

The next steps were easy. The two young hackers, who were in their teens, had done all the hacking from a local cybercafé, which at the time was well known around Romania. They confessed and explained that they used stolen credit card information obtained from the Internet black market and used the computers from the café to launch their attacks. Within several hours of debriefing the boys, they agreed to work for the Romanian police, and we financed their activities. It was fantastic, not to mention, we now looked like huge heroes. They picked up on the partnership forged between the U.S. Secret Service and Romanian police. The U.S. Embassy was excited, and I was pleased to be a part of their team.

Unlike in Rome and Bulgaria, I operated in Romania without a firearm or other weapon. This made me vulnerable. Nonetheless, as stated earlier, my Romanian counterparts were honest, hardworking law enforcement officers who protected me. They soon introduced me to Victor, who was a local up-and-coming politician and brand-new prosecutor. These men were willing and able to help me address the growing cyber concerns we had in the United States. Romanian programmers in the early 2000s were among the most sought after in the world.

As large international IT companies slowly turned to this Eastern European country, they focused on taking advantage of the strong computer and language skills coupled with cheap labor that the country provided. Yet, its computer literacy is not without its dark side. The country had, at the time, an unenviable reputation as a hotbed for computer fraud and a large community of hackers. The "legitimate" IT was one of Romania's fastest-growing export sectors. Also, roughly 90 percent, about 1,000 IT companies in Romania today, are foreign-owned, and the government hopes exports will reach 1 billion euros in the next couple of years.

At the time, no one would have realized this phenomenon, and today, Romania is the biggest single source of online fraud in the world, a multimillion-dollar industry that scams people using legitimate websites like eBay. It was very organized. They created fake accounts to trick people into thinking they were insured. If law enforcement could focus on the

Romanians and stop this activity, the amount of online fraud would drop significantly. Some experts estimate about 70 percent of software used in Romania is pirated, and that "salesmen" still visit office buildings in central Bucharest to sell pirated CDs and DVDs.

What was amazing was that many of the hackers I investigated hoped through their hacks they would be recognized and offered positions of employment with companies and/or foreign governments. The Romanian hacking community is quite large, and they basically see the computer as their "ticket out" of the country. Even today, it is still considered the easiest way to get a better-paying job abroad.

The Secret Service today, I am proud to say, has proven quite adept and successful at identifying and targeting Romanian hackers. Within the year of my presence in Romania, the Secret Service had justification for opening an office. Within no time at all, the office in Bucharest was staffed with a supervisor and an agent who spoke Romanian. Our presence was recognized, and it was time now for me to find a new mission!

## 14 Sofia, Bulgaria: Kill the Informant/Agent

It was a cold day in Bulgaria, and I sat alone in a café within a lobby of an old but luxurious hotel in downtown Sofia. As I waited patiently for an important meeting to begin, I sipped an espresso that had a terrible aftertaste. I missed the joy of drinking my cappuccino at a café in the beautiful city of Rome, where bartenders made each cup a work of art.

This particular meeting I was about to have was different from all the others while assigned in Bulgaria. For starters, I had countersurveillance support that was extended to me through Roberto, the assistant regional security officer at the American Embassy. Roberto was a friend who always supported me whenever he could. I was dressed in my usual street attire: a long, thin, black trench coat I bought in Istanbul, Turkey; jeans; and my square-toed, black biker boots. Tucked under my black, Italian-made turtleneck sweater was my .380 Sig, and on my left wrist, I wore my signature Secret Service Rolex. I appeared more like a gangster than law enforcement, but there was no doubt to those in the Bulgarian underworld who I was.

This time, I was a bit nervous. This meeting was orchestrated by Deputy Minister of Interior Boyko Borrisov, who had become a close partner in my fight to bring some sort of order and instill a semblance of genuine initiative from my counterparts in the Bulgaria National Police. I did my best to work with them and be inclusive, but this time was different. It had to be. I did not include them in my meeting, nor were they involved in any of the searches and negotiations that led up to the meeting. I had grown increasingly frustrated since arriving in Bulgaria 4 months prior. All meetings with my police counterparts were filled with empty promises and were a complete waste of time.

I had some "incentives," namely financial, in my back pocket that if and when the time was right, I could lay them on the negotiating table. I held off initially, since I knew that the moment the funds were released, I would never see any real progress or change from the police. Therefore, I played the same "cat-and-mouse" game we had engaged in for the past 4 months. Whenever I met "the three stooges," the major, the colonel, and the general, all from the police headquarters command in Sofia, I did exactly what they did. I always started by praising them. I laughed and joked with them and, in the end, provided them little to no information on what I was doing.

I knew that any lead I provided was going to be compromised. It was also obvious that most, if not all, of the counterfeit plant suppressions the police were conducting were, in my opinion, absolutely staged. Since I never suffered fools lightly, I preferred not to be involved with the "pomp and circumstance." Then from out of the blue, I received a call to meet at police headquarters. Upon arrival, I was scuffled into a room, briefed on the case, and handed a counterfeit note to examine. Ultimately, I wondered if this was just some staged occurrence.

My solution to being partnered with this corrupt group of Bulgarian law enforcement folks was to select my own team from scratch. This proved to be almost impossible to achieve, but I was stuck and needed to do something. I first teamed up with the attorneys from both the U.S. Treasury and the U.S. Department of Justice, who, like me, were assigned to the American Embassy. Their joint focus was on improving Bulgarian criminal statutes, the "rule of law," so to speak. Together, we identified the gaps in the Bulgarian criminal procedure and homed in on a strategy to fix what we could. We attempted to "decipher" the strict rules behind information sharing, and in order to do so, we met with prominent folks in all sectors of banking, finance, and security to discuss the process and a way forward.

As I began to meet these people from various government and private sector companies, I latched onto those who had similar viewpoints and were equally, if not more, frustrated with the process. These were nationals who appeared generally excited over the American presence and displayed a willingness to help improve the rule of law in their beloved country.

It was very difficult to find leaders within the group that had the ability or autonomy to demonstrate any semblance of independent thought. The main reason for this was the ever-lurking threat of repercussions they faced from their government. This obstacle, and being placed in Bulgaria, in essence, with little to no support from my own agency, made my task almost impossible. Hands down, this assignment was a huge challenge, and I was not as successful as I needed to be. This, however, did not prevent me from trying to make a difference.

I attended speaking engagements to address the areas in need of improvement. I worked with American Embassy assets and, eventually, was able to cultivate a few confidential informants. In retrospect, during my time in Bulgaria, I was unfortunately unable to find an honest investigator, which limited my progress.

My appointment was late, so I continued to sip on my bad-tasting coffee. He was known on the streets as the "Dimata Rusnaka" a.k.a. "The Russian," but his actual name was Dimitri Minev, one of the founders of SIC insurance company. The SIC organization was actually engaged in extortion, racketeering, trafficking of humans and drugs, money laundering, and other illegal activities. My meeting with Minev was about one of his earners, Petar "Peter" Simenov. Dimitri Minev was no joke. He was a very serious gangster who was associated with the Russian Mafia. He was indeed a ruthless man whose reputation for such had no equal in the criminal world of Bulgaria.

I spotted Dimitri as he exited his vehicle, an armored Mercedes SUV, trailed by another vehicle of similar make and antiballistic capacity. Several hulking bodyguards who were known to carry compact semiautomatic machine guns accompanied him. My Sig was absolutely no match. He approached the table, and I stood to shake his hand, and in almost perfect English, he greeted me and apologized for being late. Although forewarned, I was amazed at his command of English. We started with a bit of small talk. He asked me if I was able to enjoy my stay in Sofia, and how much longer I planned to stay. I used the lead by informing him that my stay depended upon when Peter

Simenov was planning to cooperate and return to the United States to face justice.

Dimitri didn't respond but rather told me how he owns property in America and how he was having issues obtaining his visa. At that moment, the waitress asked us for our order, and without hesitation, he ordered us each a shot of Rakia, which is a brandy and the national drink in Bulgaria. I hated the stuff but felt compelled to partake. While in Bulgaria, I once had a terrible sore throat, and a lady friend poured the brandy on a white T-shirt that she pulled out of my closet, and applied fresh ground black pepper to it. She applied it on my throat and within hours the relief began to kick in, as well as my energy.

Once the drink order was placed, considering the strong likelihood of someone listening in, I responded to his concern about the visa. "Dimitri," I said, "We can obviously make a case for you and will get back to you at the appropriate time." I left the issue of the visa on the table in hopes for him to see a viable exchange was possible. He was appreciative, and before I could say another word, he looked at me and asked what the need for all the security was. With a slight smirk and laugh, he followed up by saying, "Look, I know all these guys, so don't bother." I politely explained that it was embassy protocol to have them and that I had no option but to take the resources. At that moment, the waitress returned with more Rakia and Dimitri grabbed his first order and in one motion, made it disappear. I, having no choice, followed his lead, and before I was able to gasp for air, a new drink was waiting for me. I was going to be in trouble. As I'm a non-drinker, this was going to finish horribly and not in my favor.

He then leaned forward and explained how he was recently denied a visa from the American Embassy. He explained that he needed to return to the United States to take care of his personal affairs. He asked again for my assistance. I empathized with him and acknowledged the sense of urgency, but I also capitalized by raising the need to resolve the issue of the fugitive Peter Simenov. I told him, if this was resolved, then and only then could we entertain his request. To my complete surprise, he responded by saying, "Don't worry about Peter. He will do what I tell him to do."

Like that, it seemed to be done! At that moment, I heard in his voice his willingness to cooperate, and without warning, I grabbed my drink and cheered in Bulgarian, "Nazdráve!" Everyone in close proximity stopped talking and looked over to see what had happened. They realized who was in my presence and promptly returned to their business. His security folks were startled, but once they realized their boss was fine, they removed their hands from their jackets. Dimitri seemed startled too by my outburst but not only did he join in and laugh with me but also took the opportunity to toast to the idea of having an exchange take place with the "Americans" so that everyone looked good. He obviously wanted to help Boyko get in good with the Americans, he wanted his visa to enter the United States, and Peter was on his own. As far as Dimitri was concerned, this was a business deal that made complete sense. Peter, due to his own carelessness in New York, now brought attention to Dimitri, unwanted attention at that, and he needed to get his boss out of it.

Sometime later, I received an interesting phone call from a Bulgarian woman who worked tirelessly in getting her country to move in the right direction. She called me in October 2004, approximately 1 year after I left Bulgaria, and she was in shock. She said, "The news here has just reported that Dimitri was gunned down in front of his body guards in downtown Sofia." A chill went up my spine upon hearing the news.

These people were basically one step above "primitive," and they were hungry to both protect their interests, and above all, did not worry about being investigated. The police worked for them, and the prosecutors did as they were told, so no one in government was a threat. The only issue for them at this time was a quasi-political request by the Secret Service and one special agent—me—who was pushing the official request to have Simenov surrender and on his own so as to fly back with me to the United States.

* * *

My road to Bulgaria was not planned or one that I would have foreseen by any means. Outside of the gun permit I received to allow me to carry during my time in country, a paycheck, and a "safe house" to use when my cases required it, nothing more was done to secure, fund, or establish a comprehensive plan to secure my safety, or more importantly, to execute our mission in the country. We were an agency tasked with a dual mission, but when it came to investigations at that time, we simply lacked "depth." Once again, I had reached a level of frustration with my agency's lack of expertise and endurance to conduct sophisticated, long-term, financial fraud investigations.

This void resurfaced and continued to chip away at me, and I had enough of it. The overseas assignments were filled around the protection assignments, despite that there was a great deal of good work to do, but no one to do it. So, while at my desk in the Rome Field Office, I submitted my letter of resignation with the intent to work in another government agency. No sooner did I submit my letter when a disagreement occurred between a trusted colleague and myself, which resulted in me losing a friendship and my assignment in Rome. The disagreement also impacted my decision to return to the United States and work for another agency. The final outcome, since the agent replacing me was already notified, was for me to return to the Secret Service headquarters in Washington, DC, go to Sofia, Bulgaria, or go to Istanbul, Turkey.

I chose Bulgaria because I knew that the women were beautiful and that the assignment was going to be risky, and I was ready for both. Mentally, I immediately adjusted and focused on the new assignment.

In any event, the new journey began in May 2002. I was on a 2-hour Alitalia flight from Italy to Sofia, Bulgaria.

As I cleared customs, I stepped out and was struck by the cold gray air of Bulgaria. I entered the dark SUV awaiting me and was greeted by a colleague I will only identify as Michael and an embassy driver. I didn't speak a word of the Slavic language…This was going to be interesting.

As I explained in Chapter One, Sofia, Bulgaria, was not a pretty place. Sofia was a gray city, cold, and in many ways, it seemed like a place still stuck in the early Soviet era of the 1970s. Not only were the training and equipment inadequate but also the salaries paid to police officers were substandard. The average monthly salary of a Bulgarian police officer varied from 500 lev for a new police officer to 900 lev for those with extensive professional experience. The average monthly salary in Bulgaria is some 600 lev, which is approximately $300 in the United States and this gives you a great comparison of how little the police in Bulgaria are paid next to others around the world.

It reminded me of nothing back home, so for me, very little was attractive other than my job assignment. I was fortunate that many Bulgarians did speak English, and the informants who I dealt with spoke English. In other instances, I relied on a select few from the U.S. Embassy to engage my Bulgarian counterparts, but for the most part, I had to rely on my instincts and street experience to decipher who was being more truthful and whether I was being set up.

* * *

The National Police Service is responsible for combatting general crime and supporting the operations of other law enforcement agencies in Bulgaria, like the National Investigative Service and the Central Office for Combatting Organized Crime. The Police Service has criminal and financial sections across both national and local offices. They were the ones who investigated counterfeit cases. Prior to Bulgaria, I had limited exposure to counterfeit currency investigations. In Rome, we received an occasional request for support from the United States, but for the most part, it was running a suspected note through our counterfeit database, then shipping it to our headquarters for further analysis or just logging it as evidence.

When at the New York Field Office, one of the most active offices investigating counterfeit currency due to the Gotti case, I spent no time working counterfeit currency investigations. Nonetheless, it didn't matter. Counterfeit cases were worked similarly to how one would work a low-level drug case. The goal in most scenarios was to purchase through the use of an undercover operative or an informant a series of samples, thus hoping to work up the "food chain" until you have a main distributor or a possible stash house.

With counterfeit currency, the goal was to suppress the note that was being counterfeited. And most of our bosses believed that by getting to the "counterfeit plant," which was the location where the counterfeit currency was produced, meant basically the end of the investigation. Let me say, this approach might have been true in the "old days" when printing presses were used in producing currency, but in the age of computers and high-tech printers, mobility became an issue and the "art" in fabricating the counterfeit plates was removed.

The counterfeiters had minimal experience but produced a relatively high-quality product in short order. The crooks abandoned the old method, a means that required creating a negative plate of a certain denomination, then producing the actual engraved plate, which allowed the mass production of the denomination/currency. They also had to find a printing press similar to the ones used to crank out newspapers to fabricate the counterfeit money.

Once the new method of using computers and laser printers came into play, it replaced the old means and the Service was on a completely different playing field when it came to locating and dismantling an operation.

With small-sized equipment, a plant was mobile and easily transferable and became very difficult to locate.

The beginning of this book described my time in Bulgaria and how the main focus of that assignment was to locate and return to justice a fugitive, Petar Simenov. "Peter," as he was called, was a Bulgarian citizen, and in Bulgaria, the extradition of its citizens was not permissible due to the limited agreement in place between the U.S. and Bulgaria concerning such matters. Peter, upon making bail, took the first flight to Bulgaria and was never seen again.

I knew nothing about the case until the Counterfeit Division at headquarters got a hold of me and asked me to look into finding the fugitive. My boss, Ralph, the Special Agent In Charge of the Rome Field Office, felt that locating and bringing Peter Simenov to the U.S. was going to make me a "star" in the Secret Service. He knew how much I enjoyed investigations and the difficulty I had with wearing both a protection and investigative hat when both required extensive attention to detail. In his mind, the assignment would keep me focused for at least 6 months doing just criminal work.

OK, why not? Let's go get this fugitive. So I immediately went to work. The first thing was to share the warrant and all details available about him with both

Europol and Interpol. Europol was a fairly new organization at the time, but I did everything I could in notifying the appropriate authorities in order to make Peter's travels within Europe, as well as elsewhere, very difficult. I did not assume Peter was traveling under his real name. Obtaining a passport in a different name and new identity was fairly easy in Bulgaria.

I began to develop an investigative plan comprised of trusted sources. In addition to the sources, the Regional Security Officer's shop and an agency I will not mention provided assets that helped locate the fugitive. In no time at all, I began to get information that Peter was in Sofia, and that he was reporting to a Russian who ran one of the most powerful organized crime syndicates in Bulgaria: Dimitri Minev a.k.a. "The Russian." Menev was on everyone's investigative radar except the Bulgarian police. I was fortunate to have the hard-charging U.S. Ambassador James W. Pardew in country. The ambassador greatly supported U.S. law enforcement activities in Bulgaria, and with his support and that of my boss in Rome, I had every intention to contribute to the cause.

After our brief encounter in the nightclub, I met Peter at noon that very next day at the Borisova Gradina Park. It was cold, and I had added a few more layers of clothing to my standard attire: fitted black fleece gloves and a black ski hat. I stood next to the statue of Bratska Mogila as I had informed Peter where I'd be, but I was not alone. The surveillance team from the embassy was in place. Roberto was there with his team, and it wasn't long after 12 noon that I noticed from a distance the figure of the man I waited for: Peter. He saw me and without delay, joked about the location and time of the meeting. He obviously had a rough night and was still in his nightclub attire. Regardless of his condition, I got straight to the point. I identified myself, showed him my Secret Service credentials, and explained to him that it would be in his best interest to cooperate and return to the United States. He smirked and arrogantly responded by telling me he was Bulgarian and there was no extradition treaty, so I should go fuck myself. I paused and took a deep breath and upon exhaling, I explained to him that I was not going back to the U.S. without him. Again, he laughed.

Peter was conflicted. While he felt safe and secure in Bulgaria, at the same time, he also felt trapped. I needed to keep him trapped until I found a solution to the issue. I was determined to hold to my promise and only leave Bulgaria with him in tow. So for the next several months, I worked on various options in an effort to catch a break. At first, I was hopefully optimistic. The possibility of a rendition (the forcible movement of an individual from one country to another, without use of a formal legal process, such as extradition) looked promising, but after several "high-level" meetings, things began to take a turn—and not in my favor but rather for Peter's. We were able to coordinate a meeting with the prime minister. The bosses came in from Rome, and we broke the ice by complimenting the prime minister for his ability to speak Italian. It seemed to work, but after several flattering statements, he turned, and with a motionless face and in Italian so none of the Bulgarians could hear, explained that, unfortunately, there was no political will to grant such an operation. I needed to find an alternative route.

The very next week as I sat down for a one-on-one with Deputy Minister of Interior Boyko Borrisov, during our routine update meetings where we discussed various counterfeiting cases, I brought up the name Peter Simenov. I explained the case and how important this fugitive's return to the U.S. would be to our relationship. Boyko was not stupid. He saw this as an opportunity to build a stronger relationship with the United States. This was a negotiation in which he held some major cards. He needed an alliance outside of the "old," long-established relationship with mother Russia, which he was looking to balance with new ties to Washington. He quickly recommended an operation that would solve this matter. I responded by highlighting the risks associated with such an operation.

Within minutes, he was on the phone with his old cronies at SIC. Boyko was once a part of SIC. Now a wealthy man, he had turned a new leaf and focused on doing good deeds for Bulgaria. As explained, SIC was an insurance company run by the Bulgarian Mafia, and one of the founders, who was on the phone with Boyko, was Dimitri Minev. Peter reported to Minev, and Boyko was speaking to him in front of me on the ministry hard line. What the fuck! When he got off the phone, he said, "You have a meeting with Menev." Menev was aware of the situation and was willing to meet to discuss particulars.

Through the translator, I was told where to meet Menev. With that said, I had just enough time to brief the bosses, as well as prepare for the meeting. The bosses in Rome were excited, and headquarters started to get very interested, and I briefed them more and more each day. I was not worried, and I guess in some ways not concerned for whatever reason, but I was definitely now in the crosshairs. Someone or something had to give, but when and exactly where I had no clue.

As my assignment was coming to an end, I grew increasingly disillusioned with the Bulgarians. One day, I received a call from my boss in Rome. He was very vague, and in an almost dry tone, he explained how the FBI had received a call from the German police, the Bundeskriminalamt (BKA). The Germans wanted to convey some information on "our" informants in Bulgaria, and I was instructed to, when possible, coordinate my travels to meet them.

I contacted the Secret Service agent assigned at Interpol who was coordinating the meeting. So I flew to Germany and headed straight to the city of Wiesbaden where the headquarters for the BKA were located. The folks there were all very quiet and with a look of surprise, asked me if I was the agent living in Bulgaria. I responded yes, as I proudly displayed my Secret Service credentials and diplomatic passport. The meeting started with them handing me transcripts of an intercepted conversation between a Bulgarian Mafia figure they were targeting and an unknown Bulgarian living in Sofia. The conversation pertained to growing frustration with certain factions of the Mafia in Bulgaria. Whatever the issue, the order was passed, and it was very clear: ***Kill the informant and if you can, kill the agent as well.***

My mouth dropped, I had really nothing to say. I was alone, and now, armed with this information, I was in deep trouble. Upon my return to Sofia, I immediately stopped all communication with the informants and halted all meetings with the Bulgarian authorities with the exception of Boyko. I spoke with Boyko and told him of the threat, minus who gave me the information. I was furious, to say the least, and so was he.

Boyko was crushed upon hearing the news. We had gotten along well, and he was frustrated. He knew this was not a good thing, in particular as it related to his relationship with the U.S. ambassador and his desire to forge a strong partnership with the U.S.

I briefed other assets that week, and on Sunday morning, while having breakfast at the Hilton Restaurant with others from the embassy, I was interrupted from eating by two hulking men. They asked me to accompany them to the Ministry of Interior for a very sensitive meeting. I was wearing my Adidas workout gear and sneakers. Unshaven and wearing a baseball cap, I asked if I could go to my apartment to get properly dressed. With no hesitation, the two gorillas said, "No." I looked at my friends and wondered what this was but placed trust in the men to being who they said they were. Rob knew what to do. He called the local assets, and before I got off the hotel elevator and in the car with them, it was confirmed that this was a legitimate meeting. A text message from one of the folks in a certain agency gave me assurances that this was legitimate.

Boyko was at one end of his table, a long one that could seat all his generals, if need be. On one side of that table, Boyko's left, sat a general, a colonel, and a major, all known to me and to the Secret Service. I was on the other side of the table, Boyko's right. Standing behind the general was the translator. She began to translate, and it was not good news. Boyko was angry. At one point, he was actually screaming at the top of his lungs, upset by the latest news he heard of his guest (me) being threatened. As I sat there, I hoped that nothing had happened to my informants and realized that from this point forward, until I left this country, I now had an even bigger bull's-eye on my back. As far as the informants, these 9 months spending countless hours with both, I began to grow close to them and saw them a bit differently, which, of course, could be dangerous.

I looked down at the table in front of me, sort of the same way my son now would do when being reprimanded. I just couldn't look at them. That is, until the one in the middle, the colonel, began to cry. He was, in my opinion, the least corrupt and genuinely wanted me to date his daughter and possibly take her away from Bulgaria to give her a better life. He had lived a life filled with corruption, deception, and death, and may have wanted his daughter to escape the exposure to it. My courage returned, and as the words spewed out of Boyko's mouth, I looked up at each and every one of those men straight in their eyes, and after it was all over, they were told to submit their resignations. On those words, they stood at attention and saluted Boyko. The colonel looked at me, and with tears in his eyes, said in broken English, "Sorry, Nino, sorry, Nino." I just looked and within seconds, they had emptied the room.

My time in Bulgaria was over, and as I boarded my flight back to the U.S., with a quick connection in Frankfurt, Germany, I was handed a gift from Deputy Minister of Interior Boyko Borrisov, who accompanied me to the runway in his personal armored vehicle. The gift was an exact replica sword of the one worn by King Ferdinand I of Bulgaria. I was shocked, and as he walked off the plane, his motorcade waiting and men dressed in ceremonial uniforms, saluting, he turned with one last wave and departed the runway.

## 15 More About the Author

Nino Perrotta has more than 25 years of experience in military, security, and protective services. His expertise includes threat analysis/mitigation, physical and facility security, major event logistics, and VIP travel. Nino has successfully conducted complex investigations domestically and abroad.

In 1990, after receiving his army commission from Fordham University, Nino embarked on his military training at Fort Huachuca, Arizona. There, he completed both the officer basic military intelligence training and advance counterintelligence training, which resulted in his appointment as a counterintelligence officer, United States Army Reserves.

In 1993, he began his career in law enforcement as one of the first "all-civilian" investigators for Mayor David Dinkins' newly created New York City Civilian Complaint Review Board (CCRB). The CCRB's mission was to investigate, mediate, make findings, and recommend courses of action on complaints against New York City police officers. These complaints often alleged the use of excessive or unnecessary force, abuse of authority, or discourtesy toward the public.

In 1994, after completing the Rockland County Police Academy, Nino was assigned to the Bronx County District Attorney's (DA) Detective Investigators Bureau. During his tenure at the DA's office, Nino investigated gambling and loan sharking activities of Gambino crime family "soldier" Greg DePalma. Through Nino's leadership, tenacity, and superior investigative skills, the investigation expanded. Prior to Nino's departure to the United States Secret Service in 1995, the investigation was ready to target the head of the Gambino crime family, John A. Gotti Junior.

After a tour at the Secret Service's New York Field Office, where Nino investigated numerous financial and electronic crimes, he was assigned to the field office in Rome, Italy.

While overseas, Nino conducted numerous protective security advances for both the president and former presidents of the United States. Nino also worked closely with the Italian authorities on fraud, financial, and cybercrime investigations with global implications.

Nino collaborated with the Italian Finance Police (Guardia di Finanza) on one such investigation which identified a scheme in Pescara, Italy. The perpetrators,

Italian university professors, were defrauding the city of Pescara with a sophisticated prime bank lending scheme posing as members of the U.S. Federal Reserve Bank who claimed unrealistic returns on government investments.

Nino was then assigned to Bucharest, Romania, to address the growth of computer hacking and fraud cases against U.S. companies and government agencies.

In Romania, Nino continued conducting high-impact, successful investigations that led to the prosecution of numerous Romanian criminals. Nino leveraged this success to establish a mutually beneficial relationship between Romania and the Secret Service. These cooperative efforts with the Romanian authorities helped justify the funding and establishment of a permanent Secret Service presence in the country.

After his tenure in Romania, Nino was sent to Sophia, Bulgaria for a 9-month assignment to replicate his success in Romania; namely, to establish a Secret Service office in Bulgaria. He quickly went to work establishing liaisons and partnerships with Bulgarian law enforcement and the private sector.

Nino also coordinated investigations to combat counterfeiting of U.S. currency. One case involved

Nino successfully tracking, locating, and apprehending a fugitive, who fled the U.S. for Bulgaria after being indicted by the Secret Service in New York for counterfeit currency violations.

Nino obtained the trust and confidence of senior-ranking officials in the Bulgarian Ministry of Interior. In 2002, along with the support of the American Embassy, he established, in Bulgaria, the first "international" Secret Service Electronic Crimes Task Force (ECTF).

In 2003, upon the conclusion of his foreign tour of duty, Nino represented the Secret Service at the newly created U.S. Department of Homeland Security National Operations Center (NOC) in Washington, DC.

At the NOC, Nino helped deliver real-time situational awareness and monitored homeland defense and security issues. He successfully worked with governors, homeland security advisors, law enforcement partners, and critical infrastructure operators in all 50 states and 50+ major urban areas nationwide. Nino went on to become the assistant senior watch officer, Office of the Under Secretary, responsible for the coordination, collection, and fusion of information from more than 35 federal, state, territorial, tribal, local, and private sector agencies.

Since 2004, Nino has been a Senior Special Agent with a United States government agency.

In addition to an accomplished professional career, Nino holds a BA and MA in political science from Fordham University, New York, New York. He is also a graduate of both the Federal Law Enforcement Training Center, Glynco, Georgia, and the United States Secret Service Academy, Laurel, Maryland.

Some noteworthy awards bestowed upon Nino include:

- Special award for prosecution of Seynabou Seck in the Southern District of New York and the prime bank lending scheme in Pescara, Italy.
- New York State Law Enforcement Award for investigation and prosecution of John A. Gotti and the Gambino crime family.
- FBI award for investigation into European-American Bank robberies.

Nino is an accomplished hunter who loves the outdoors, and in 2012, he sold a successful start-up construction company based in Washington, DC that he founded in 2004. Today, he is the proud owner of Sequoia Security Group, Inc. based in Washington, DC.

**Figure 1:** Nino Perrotta at West Point, New York during his Fordham Army ROTC days, 1988 – 1989.

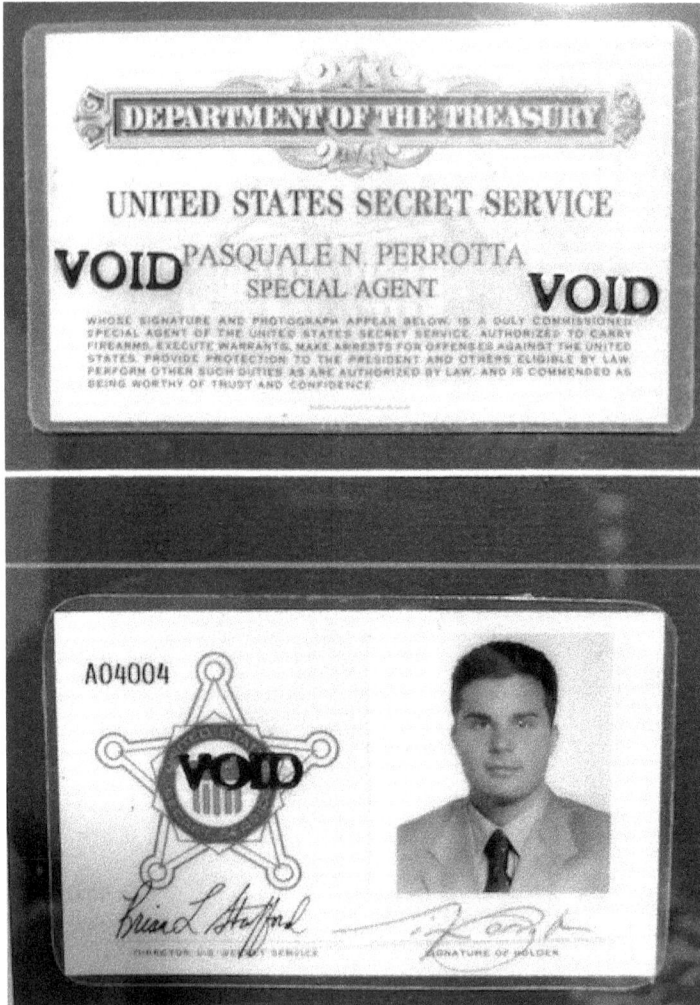

**Figure 2:** Special Agent Nino Perrotta, U.S. Secret Service Badge.

**Figure 3:** A ceremony acknowledging various individual investigative accomplishments. SAIC Brian Gimlett (far left); DSAIC Chip Smith (far right). A proud moment being publicly recognized for my contribution towards the Gotti "Junior" investigation.

**Figure 4:** Secret Service Special Agent Nino Perrotta; Mary Jo White, The United States attorney for the Southern District of New York from 1993 to 2002; Special Agent Walter Carroll, FBI; Detective Tom Buda, NYPD. Receiving awards for the Commodore Investigation, SDNY.

185

**Figure 5:** Special Agent Nino Perrotta
going to work in his work clothes.

**Figure 6:** SA Nino Perrotta holding evidence of various prepaid calling cards
involved in the $94 million scheme.

**Figure 7:** Special Agent Nino Perrotta; ATSAIC Robert Weaver; and Special Agent Chris Funk. Nino jokingly cuffs Weaver after completing a successful undercover operation against a mob associate, who was involved in the prepaid phone card scam.

**Figure 8:** ATSAIC Marty Walsh and SA Nino Perrotta in front of the building where John Gotti "Junior" ran his prepaid phone card operation.

**Figure 9:** The Gotti Search Warrant Team.

*Dual Mission* is a memoir of Special Agent Nino Perrotta of the United States Secret Service. Perrotta's relentless law enforcement efforts helped take down John Gotti Junior, the leader of the Gambino crime family, and Cy Young Award winning MLB pitcher Denny McLain, who among a vast criminal network scammed hard-working immigrants and tele-communications companies out of nearly a hundred million dollars.

## About the Author

Nino Perrotta is the son of Italian immigrant parents who came to New York in search of the American dream. Special Agent Perrotta's law enforcement career spanned 25 years and involved international missions in Italy, Romania, and Bulgaria. Today he is a successful security consultant in the Washington metropolitan region.

www.ingramcontent.com/pod-product-compliance
Lightning Source LLC
Chambersburg PA
CBHW041256040426

42334CB00028BA/3045